Leading Powerful Professional Learning

Leading Powerful Professional Learning

Responding to Complexity With Adaptive Expertise

Deidre Le Fevre

Helen Timperley

Kaye Twyford

Fiona Ell

Foreword by Viviane Robinson

A Joint Publication

FOR INFORMATION:

CORWIN
A SAGE Company
2455 Teller Road
Thousand Oaks, California 91320
(800) 233-9936
www.corwin.com

SAGE Publications Ltd.
1 Oliver's Yard
55 City Road
London EC1Y 1SP
United Kingdom

SAGE Publications India Pvt. Ltd.
B 1/I 1 Mohan Cooperative Industrial Area
Mathura Road, New Delhi 110 044
India

SAGE Publications Asia-Pacific Pte. Ltd.
18 Cross Street #10-10/11/12
China Square Central
Singapore 048423

Printed in the United States of America

ISBN 978-1-5443-6145-1

Program Director and Publisher:
    Dan Alpert
Content Development Editor:
    Lucas Schleicher
Senior Editorial Assistant: Mia Rodriguez
Project Editor: Amy Schroller
Copy Editor: Megan Markanich
Typesetter: Hurix Digital
Proofreader: Ellen Brink
Indexer: Jean Casalegno
Cover and Graphic Designer:
    Dally Verghese
Marketing Manager: Sharon Pendergast

This book is printed on acid-free paper.

Certified Chain of Custody
Promoting Sustainable Forestry
www.sfiprogram.org
SFI-01268
SFI label applies to text stock

19 20 21 22 23 10 9 8 7 6 5 4 3 2 1

Contents

Visit the companion website at
https://resources.corwin.com/LeadingPowerfulPL
for downloadable resources.

Foreword

A profound shift is taking place in the design, delivery, and evaluation of professional learning (PL) for teachers and leaders. The criteria for success are no longer that participants are energized and enthused by their PL experiences. We know that such motivational outcomes are not sufficient for changes in practice. Even changes in practice, subsequent to a PL experience, may not be an adequate measure of success, for we know that in our world of educational fads and fashions, leaders and teachers can conscientiously change their practice in ways that make no difference to, or even harm, the learning of their students.

The new criterion for the effectiveness of PL is that it changes leader and teacher practice in ways that make a positive difference to the learning and well-being of their students. This is what Le Fevre and her coauthors call powerful PL. In short, the shift is from an adult-centered to a more student-centered approach to the evaluation of PL.

Creating a school culture of formal and informal student-centered PL is about the most important thing a leader can do. In a meta-analysis of the effects of five different sets of leadership practices, promoting and participating in PL had the largest average effect on student outcomes (Robinson, 2011; Robinson, Lloyd, & Rowe, 2008). Using a very different methodology, economists of education have also established strong links between such leadership and student outcomes. I refer specifically to the work of Helal and Coelli (2016), who, in a longitudinal study of the impact of principal turnover on student progress from Years 3 to 5, found that the two key pathways through which principals made an impact on student outcomes were promotion of goal congruence and teacher professional interaction and growth.

Recent research, including that by some of the authors of this book, has also provided considerable insight into the mechanisms responsible for the link between the leadership of PL and student outcomes. First, investment in PL is more likely to benefit the students of the participating teachers if leaders make strategic decisions about the focus of PL. Decisions are strategic when priorities for PL are based on examination of a range of evidence about which students have and have not progressed at the appropriate rate. This evidence tells leaders what they and their teachers have yet to learn in order to close the gaps for these students. Strategic choice ensures, therefore, that the focus and content of PL for the adults is strongly aligned to the learning needs of their students. Some of the leadership practices involved are described and illustrated in Chapter 3 in the Purpose and Focus section.

Second, teacher PL is more likely to benefit students if it is evidence based in its content and process. The content is evidence based when there is a valid theory describing how and why the approach improves student outcomes and strong evidence that it does so. The requirement for evidence-based content applies whether the PL is developed in house or based on an externally developed program. In the latter case, leaders who are mindful of the need for evidence-based content can access increasingly sophisticated websites that summarize the results of well-designed evaluation studies of a range of PL programs in many different subject areas (www.evidenceforessa.org; https://educationendowmentfoundation.org.uk/evidence-summaries).

Leaders who ask questions about evidence of impact, even in the face of enthusiastic advocacy of a particular program, package, or innovation, are more likely to see their investment in PL payoff in terms of improved student outcomes.

PL needs an evidence-based process as well as evidence-based content because research generalizations about the overall impact of a PL program provide probabilities rather than guarantees of impact in any particular setting. Continuous inquiry into the implementation of a program is needed to monitor progress and make those adjustments to the context and to the program that are needed for success.

The inquiry process is even more critical when leading PL that is not based on a proven program—when leaders and teachers come together to examine evidence of student need, generate and test hypotheses about school-based contributors to the learning gaps, and then craft and test ways to address those gaps. In this type of PL, the relevant evidence is located in the practice of teachers, in the response of their students, and in the artifacts that they each produce. This book provides rich explanations and illustrations of the dispositions and skills needed to lead such inquiry.

Third, PL is more likely to make an impact when it is narrow and deep rather than wide and shallow. A teacher PL agenda that is based on evidence of student need challenges leaders and teachers by signaling problems of practice that they have yet to understand and resolve. A safe and collaborative culture is needed where there is time to learn by taking risks, experimenting, making mistakes, and trying again and again. If adaptive expertise is to be developed, learning at the level of tips and tricks will not suffice because the learning is not anchored in deep theoretical understanding of the conditions required for improvement. Theory and practice need to be strongly connected so teachers know not only what to do but why. If they do not know the theory that explains the links between the details of their practice and the likely or actual impact on their students, they may adjust their practice in ways that reduce rather than increase the probability of making an impact on their students. A narrow and deep learning agenda communicates a seriousness of purpose by enabling an intensive and persistent focus on one main thing. It encourages iterative cycles of inquiry, action, and evaluation and reduces the distractions that come with an overcrowded learning agenda.

The fourth mechanism required for powerful PL is teacher collaboration. Why is learning through collaborative processes so popular at present? What makes it more powerful than learning on one's own? Of course, these two forms of learning are not mutually exclusive, but why the current focus on collaboration? One powerful answer is that collaboration is more likely than solitary learning to foster critical reflection on one's taken-for-granted assumptions about teaching and learning. For example, the math teacher who controls her tenth-grade algebra class by providing worksheets and quizzes rather than rich texts has, over the years, developed a strongly held and largely tacit theory about how to manage this group of students. Such theories are unlikely to be questioned by solitary reflection, for the same beliefs that inform the teacher's practice (rich texts are too hard for the students; they don't have the literacy skills needed to decode them and will misbehave if they can't do the work) will inform the teacher's reflections on her practice. Collaboration, on the other hand, enables teachers to share their different theories of action and inquire into their relative merit. A diversity of thinking about how to teach this math class provides a resource for critique and for crafting alternatives.

Whether the diverse views present in a professional learning community (PLC) are articulated, listened to, and used to test tacit theories about how to teach is largely dependent on the skill of those leading the professional community—skills that are outlined in rich detail in this book in the Effective Learning Processes section. One of the most important of these skills is the ability to foster inquiry into the connections between participants' specific teaching practices and the relevant understandings and misunderstandings of their students. When teachers talk about students' behavior or learning, without considering their own possible impact on those outcomes, skilled leaders can redirect such talk to inquire into possible links between how they were taught and what happened to students. Similarly, when teachers talk in PLCs about the teaching resources and strategies they have used, without considering their impact on students, skilled facilitators can help them inquire into those links. This type of talk builds teachers' agency and impact by building accurate self-awareness and enhancing their commitment to continuous improvement of student outcomes (www.aitsl.edu.au/tools-resources/resource/literature-review--professional-conversations-and-improvement-focused-feedback).

The authors describe their book as a resource for leaders of PL—not necessarily to be read from cover to cover but to be used as a guide to those aspects of the leadership of PL about which readers are curious, puzzled, or need to know more. The structure of the book lends itself very well to such treatment, for the various components of their model can be accessed through the detailed table of contents and through the visual representations of their model. The model incorporates a clear value base that is strongly aligned to the twelve deliberate acts of facilitation (DAFs) that constitute and promote adaptive expertise.

The leadership of PL is a powerful form of leadership. This book is an important resource for the development of such leadership.

—Viviane Robinson
Distinguished Professor, Faculty of Education and Social Work
Academic Director, Centre for Educational Leadership
University of Auckland, New Zealand

Preface

At its best, education has the power to transform lives. It can improve people's life chances, change their worldviews, lift them from poverty, and support their journies to inventing something new and revolutionary. Education can also reproduce inequity, entrench social divides, alienate people, and set people on a journey to never fulfilling their potential. Education—and educators—are powerful, powerful people.

A common goal for those of us who work in education is that we want to make a difference—we mean a positive difference. We want to contribute something to making education a force for good in our societies and a means by which society's increasing inequity can be reversed. We want to do something to help. This can be harder than we think. Education institutions tend to reproduce themselves over time, establishing ways of working and being that transcend generations of staff who work in them. New teachers tend to teach like those who taught them: it's what they know, it's what education *should* look like—and it worked for them. Indeed, people who want to help education institutions and the leaders and teachers within them to work in new ways that address inequity and produce better outcomes for learners are engaged in complex and difficult work.

This book is intended to be a resource for people who are working to make change in education settings. It is about an approach to working on improvement that is rooted in curiosity, respect, self-knowledge, and a deep understanding of the role of language and culture in education. It is an approach to the facilitation of change for improvement that brings together many parts of the task into a powerful concept: that of adaptive expertise. Adaptive expertise is a way to characterize educational professionalism that emphasizes responsiveness, relationships, and a deep knowledge base from which to make decisions.

The model and metaphor presented in this book are the result of a multiyear, collaborative research project undertaken by a research team and a group of effective facilitators who worked in schools to improve outcomes for learners. More information about the research project is available in the Research Appendix of this book.

This book is designed to make ideas quick to access and easy to use. This does not mean that the ideas themselves are simple—the task of working with other people to improve outcomes for learners can never be that—but we hope it means you can readily start thinking about the ideas and playing with them in your practice, sharing them with others, and using them as tools to make the difference you want to make.

Acknowledgments

As authors we would like to acknowledge the large group of people who, across many years, have contributed to the insights that are recorded in this book. We remain grateful to the many teachers and leaders in schools, the facilitators they worked with, and our team of researchers who willingly participated in the research projects and continually challenged us to make a difference for our learners. We thank the schools and principals, middle leaders, and teachers who participated in the research projects that inform this work and who gave us access to the multiple sides of the story about what works to make change in schools. Your perspectives enhanced our understanding of facilitation.

We would particularly like to acknowledge our colleagues at the University of Auckland who were part of the research team over the years—in particular, Rae Siʻilata, who made substantial contributions to our thinking on linguistic and cultural responsiveness (LCR) and kept us firmly focused on improving equity; Kane Meissel, who kept the quantitative work on student achievement happening; and Sarah Mayo, our research assistant and writing coach.

We wish to acknowledge the professional learning (PL) facilitators who participated in the various research projects for providing us with a window into their complex world of facilitation in action. We appreciate their willingness to share their practice and vulnerability with us without hesitation, allowing us to share our interpretations of their work with others. We hope you have learned as much as we have. Your contributions have been hugely influential on our thinking about effective facilitation, and the frameworks they have provided put the "wisdom of practice" in a wider theoretical context that enhances our findings.

We are grateful to the leadership team of the Consortium for Professional Learning (CPL), who has supported us to understand and learn more about effective facilitation. We acknowledge the individual organizations that made up CPL: the Faculty of Education and Social Work at the University of Auckland, New Zealand, and their partners Evaluation Associates, and Learning Media. We also acknowledge the wider funding provided by the New Zealand Ministry of Education for funding the work of the consortium.

To Dan Alpert, our editor, who believed that our work is important and that it could have international appeal and to Lucas Schleicher and the rest of the team at Corwin, your unrelenting positivity and calmness made the publishing process accessible to us. We wholeheartedly thank the team of reviewers who provided us with honest feedback on what worked and where we needed to improve. The final manuscript is so much better—thank you.

Publisher's Acknowledgments

Corwin gratefully acknowledges the contributions of the following reviewers:

Amy Colton
Executive Director
Learning Forward Michigan
Ann Arbor, MI

Robert Evans, EdD
Director of Teaching and Learning
American International School of Johannesburg
Johannesburg, South Africa

Terri Iles
Executive Director
Learning Forward Texas
Roanoke, TX

Joellen Killion
Senior Advisor
Learning Forward
Lakeway, TX

Eric Lee
Director
Jacksonville State University Inservice Center
Anniston, AL

Delores Lindsey
Retired Professor
California State University San Marcos
San Marcos, CA

Bryan McDonald
Assistant Professor
University of Central Missouri
Warrensburg, MO

Ron Wahlen
Director of Digital Teaching and Learning
Durham Public Schools
Durham, NC

About the Authors

Dr. Deidre Le Fevre is a senior lecturer and head of graduate programs in educational leadership at the University of Auckland. She began her career as an elementary school teacher in New Zealand and the United Kingdom before completing her PhD (Ann Arbor, MI) and moving into research and teaching at Washington State University. She has led large-scale research projects investigating effective leadership and PL practices for educational change and improvement. Her research publications focus on practices that support leaders and facilitators, improve their interpersonal effectiveness, and solve complex problems. She brings knowledge and skills in understanding organizational change, the development of professional capability, and effective leadership to her work consulting with leaders and organizations.

Dr. Helen Timperley is professor emeritus of education at The University of Auckland. Her extensive research experience has focused on how to promote professional and leadership learning in schools in ways that make a difference to outcomes for those student learners who are currently underserved by the system. She has numerous research articles in both of these areas published in international journals; has spoken at a range of invited seminars; and undertaken consultancies in Europe, Canada, and Australia. She has written six books on her specialty research areas with many translated into a range of languages. Most of her published and consultancy work has focused on school and system change through PL, professional conversations with impact, and evaluative thinking in educational innovation.

Dr. Kaye Twyford is an experienced school leader and teacher and, more recently, researcher. She is a lecturer at the University of Auckland. She also works as a consultant supporting communities of learning to build collaborative practice to raise student outcomes. Kaye completed her PhD in education (2016), investigating teachers' engagement in PL through a risk lens focused on uncertainty and vulnerability. Her work identifies the importance of reframing teacher resistance as perceptions of risk and highlights implications for mitigating risks in change. She brings knowledge and skills in project management, leading change, and collaborative inquiry.

Dr. Fiona Ell is an associate professor and head of teacher education at the University of Auckland. She has a background in elementary teaching and remains a registered teacher. Fiona's research centers on mathematics education and teacher PL, both before certification and afterward. She has worked in Australia and New Zealand on schooling improvement projects, helping schools use the spiral of inquiry to improve the learning and well-being of their students. Fiona is interested in how teachers learn about the impact of their practice from considering the responses of their learners, especially when they work with marginalized communities.

Introduction

Education can be a powerful agent of change, but too often it does not realize its potential to transform the lives of every learner. Leading, teaching, and learning occur in a complex landscape, where policy, research, history, experiences, and communities shape practice. Too often past experience as a student overrides knowledge about effective teaching. Similarly, leaders' decisions are based as much on personal experience as on formal knowledge of leadership. Practice is taken for granted, and not enough attention is given to the impact of educators' choices on learner outcomes. For example, we know that there is strong evidence for the impact of practices such as formative assessment, but formative assessment techniques are difficult for schools to establish and sustain. Leaders and teachers are hardworking and highly skilled, so why is it so difficult to lead and sustain improvement in education settings?

Teaching and learning are complex processes, and education settings are complex entities. It is tempting to think of teaching and learning as well as education settings as merely complicated. There are many students, teachers, leaders, agencies, spaces, and policies involved in education, and teaching and learning can seem like a complicated jigsaw of people and things that fit together to form the education landscape. Thinking of teaching and learning as a complicated process suggests that you can take the jigsaw apart, study or change a piece of it, and reform it into a new picture. When faced with so many contributing factors it is understandable to want to simplify them in this way. The trouble is that teaching and learning and education settings themselves are not complicated but complex. This means that linear cause-and-effect thinking, simplifying, and picking apart of processes or problems cannot result in sustained change and improvement. The complexity of teaching and learning—and the settings in which they occur—demands that leaders at all levels of education work in ways that embrace and consider this complexity as a fundamental condition of addressing education challenges to improve learner outcomes. Responding to them requires adaptive and responsive leadership, which comes from a place of curiosity and open-mindedness about solutions. How can leadership of this sort be developed in all educators in order to tackle the seemingly intractable challenges that education faces in the increasingly diverse, globalized, high-tech, and rapidly changing world?

Professional learning (PL) forms the core of all efforts to meet these challenges and to improve learner outcomes, whether at the district, school, or teacher level. Educators' own experience may not be enough to help them understand other people, their needs, values, and aspirations. They may not have the specialist knowledge needed to understand the problems they face in enough depth to solve them. They may not understand the impact of their own culture and background on the way they lead, teach, and learn, and they may struggle to be responsive to their students' different cultures, languages, and socioeconomic circumstances. PL can help with these things.

Traditional approaches to PL have not been effective in creating and sustaining change that leads to long-term improvement. Leaders and teachers work in complex and uncertain environments, constantly making decisions with only bits of information under time pressure. For PL to affect moment-by-moment interactions in schools or classrooms, it needs to be contextualized, relevant, authentic, and respectful of professional expertise. This is a challenge for leaders of PL, who are themselves an integral part of the complex web of people and events that constitute education settings. What is needed is a way of approaching PL, and the work of teaching, as complex, adaptive, context dependent, culturally located, and driven by effective decision-making. In this book we call this way of working adaptive expertise. It is a new way to think about teacher professionalism and the leading of learning to solve complex education problems.

Professionalism as Adaptive Expertise

Solving complex problems in uncertain and changing environments requires adaptive rather than routine expertise. Rather than seeing leaders and teachers as enactors of routines or following generic teaching approaches or instructions, a lens of adaptive expertise sees effective educators as responding in the moment, using their knowledge of the curriculum and individual students, while keeping a sharp eye on the consequences of their choice of teaching approaches on accelerating or deepening learning. Adaptive expertise demands in-depth knowledge and skills, being flexible and responsive to the cultures and languages of their students, and not feeling the need to subscribe to preconceived ideas about what effective teaching means. Choices made by educators with adaptive expertise are appropriate to their context, based on evidence of student learning and development, informed by deep knowledge, and evaluated for their effectiveness. These choices deliberately address inequity and are focused on making a difference for each student.

There are elements of teaching and learning that require the enactment of routine expertise because they are important in creating an orderly environment. Many of them are effective. However, one of the key differences between those educators demonstrating adaptive rather than routine expertise is that they constantly question if a particular routine is benefiting the learning of students rather than assuming that what has worked in the past will be effective for the students they now teach. The same issues apply to school and district leaders. Those with an adaptive expertise orientation ask themselves: "Does a given policy or way of doing things directly enhance teaching and learning?" "Do all those reporting requirements really lead to improved educational experiences or do they satisfy some noneducational demand that has become irrelevant over time?"

Thinking about professionalism as adaptive expertise makes new and different demands on those responsible for facilitating or leading PL. An adaptive expertise perspective means that all educators need support to be able to understand what is happening in their context for their learners (who might be young people, teachers, teacher leaders, middle leaders, principals, or system leaders). These facilitators and leaders need to have the knowledge and skills to make productive in-the-moment decisions about how best to promote PL and to evaluate what difference their actions are making. Leaders of PL have a sophisticated and difficult task as they help others learn to work in this way—and they themselves will need to work using adaptive expertise in order to support deep learning for all their learners.

The Elements of Adaptive Expertise

This book is about the facilitation of PL in ways that are consistent with the key attributes of adaptive expertise. Such expertise can be developed with the participating educators only if the facilitation of their learning is also consistent with the key attributes of adaptive expertise. This is a challenging task. So we have presented the elements of adaptive expertise in PL through the metaphor of a tree. Metaphors help us to explore and understand new ways of thinking and working. They also help us to make connections and remember the complex interlinking of thinking and action when making those important in-the-moment decisions.

Looking at Figure 1 you will notice three main parts to the tree: (1) the roots, (2) the trunk, and (3) the branches or leaves. These three parts represent the main components of adaptive expertise and the PL designed to develop it.

The roots of the tree represent the personal qualities and dispositions that underpin adaptive expertise. In the PL research on which this book is based, it became clear that these roots informed all the decisions of those facilitating the PL and were ways of being. The roots nourish the whole process and feed the in-the-moment decisions and actions of the trunk and branches or leaves.

The trunk of the tree, grounded by the roots, brings together these personal qualities and dispositions to create a core of responsiveness through relationships with a generative improvement orientation. Responsiveness refers to all learners but particularly the student learners because the ultimate goal should always be improvement in outcomes for every student. These outcomes should not be limited to academic progress and achievement but may also include well-being or other outcomes valued by the students and communities in which these students live and learn.

Responsiveness is not possible without relationships that ultimately support or constrain the effectiveness of the PL. Engagement in PL for improvement in student outcomes does not happen in the absence of strong relationships.

We have referred to improvement in the trunk in terms of generative improvement because it captures the notion that improvement is ongoing and evolves rather than being static with a fixed end point. The focus shifts as progress is made, new challenges present themselves, and the need for new learning emerges. Generative improvement also captures the idea that improvement itself generates the energy to make things better and to seek equity in valued outcomes for learners.

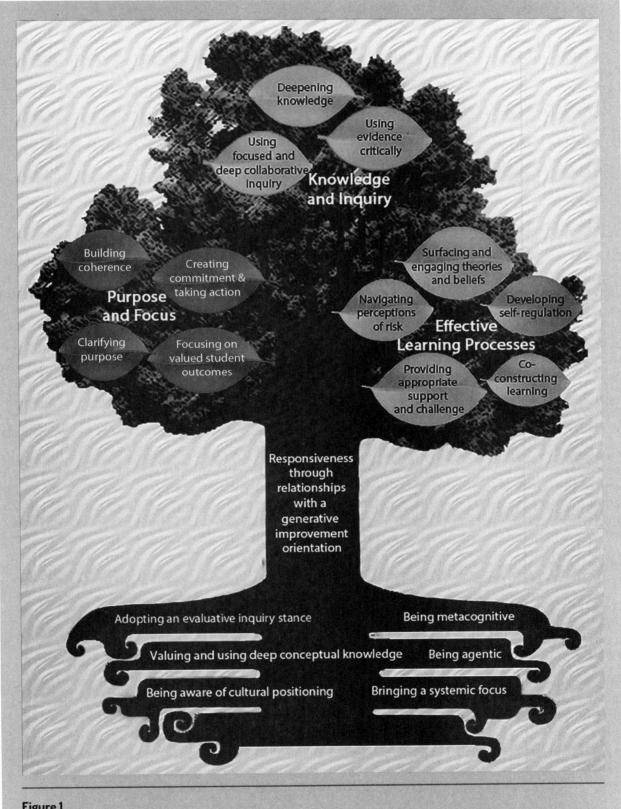

Figure 1

At the top, the branches and leaves represent the practices or actions of those facilitating PL and ultimately those participating in it as they develop adaptive expertise. They flourish as a result of strong roots and a robust trunk. The branches and leaves are not intended as a checklist of behaviors or skills to master but rather present productive facilitation choices and actions as part of an organic whole. The leaves are grouped into three branches of associated actions: (1) purpose and focus, (2) knowledge and inquiry, and (3) effective learning processes. At the more detailed level, the leaves represent deliberate actions that those leading PL can take in order to promote learning and adaptive expertise.

Throughout the book there is an intentional focus on what adaptive expertise looks like when working to improve outcomes for students from different cultures who use a range of languages. This focus places learners' identity, language, and culture central to the improvement work rather than a supplementary element to be added. As the student population becomes more diverse, the way educators approach their roles must become more responsive to this diversity.

Implications for Leaders

PL is often directed at teachers, particularly if the content focuses on teaching practices to promote student learning or well-being. On the surface, this approach appears to be logical because teachers have the greatest direct impact on student learning. Yet the research is clear; leaders who promote and participate in teacher PL and development have twice the effect size of other leadership activities. Leadership involvement is also essential for sustainability of improved outcomes because leaders create the conditions for teachers to build their adaptive expertise through working together to focus on becoming more responsive and effective for every learner. Teachers cannot do this alone.

It is also clear, however, that many leaders are reluctant to engage with teachers in new PL, and many do not have the necessarily knowledge and skills to do so. Leadership and leadership development are seen as something different from working with teachers to improve outcomes for students. The same situation often exists for district and policy leaders. They perceive it to be their job to determine the relevant policies, content, and approaches to PL and development rather than to engage with new learning directly themselves. Yet they too rarely experience the hands-on learning about how to develop the kinds of adaptive expertise appropriate to their roles.

It can be helpful to think of educators in a system as having a class. Teachers have classes of students, school leaders have classes of teachers, district leaders have classes of school leaders, and so on. In an adaptive expertise framing, the primary job of leadership at each of these levels is to teach their classes of educators, so they, in turn, can teach their classes more effectively. At every level of the system, they are likely to have diverse learners who may or may not want to engage in further learning and may be ambivalent about what it all means. This is a challenging task for many leaders. One of the authors of this book has observed the following:

> One of the greatest challenges leaders face is to overcome resistance and to increase the motivation for teachers to engage in deep professional learning. A focus on students together with a vision for new possibilities . . . becomes a central leadership role. Most important . . . is to provide the kinds of opportunities that will realize the vision.

(Timperley, 2011, p. 128)

For this reason, this book is for all educators who are responsible for the learning of their classes, whether these classes are other educators or student learners. In this leadership capacity, it demands developing the personal qualities described in the roots, being responsive through relationships with a generative improvement orientation in the trunk, and engaging in the kinds of actions described in the branches and leaves.

Just as it is no longer expected that teachers will teach in isolation, this orientation to leadership does not mean that leaders must teach their classes alone. No one has all the expertise required. Teaching one's class may be most effective in collaboration with other leaders or those with specialist expertise.

Using This Book

This book is a guide for those responsible for leading or facilitating PL in the current educational landscape that demands adaptive expertise to solve the complex education challenges everyone faces. It is based on a multiyear research project that investigated the practice of successful facilitators of PL. The book describes the components of adaptive expertise, how they apply to the leadership of PL, and how they apply to leaders and teachers who are undertaking PL. Through vignettes and excerpts from practice, links to research, and clear descriptions, the book identifies orientations, ways of working responsively, and deliberate acts of facilitation (or DAFs) that constitute adaptive expertise in PL.

Each chapter unpacks part of the tree metaphor: the roots, the trunk, and the branches. To make the ideas accessible, one-page summaries of key ideas are presented first, followed by practice-focused descriptions and examples interwoven with research on why they matter. Vignettes bring the ideas to life and help readers to see how the idea of adaptive expertise in the facilitation of PL could be applied to their own education settings.

There is no need to start this book at the beginning and finish at the end. The book is intended to be used in responsive, dynamic ways according to the challenges of a particular situation. Adaptive expertise means taking responsibility for searching for information needed at a specific time. Learning is rarely linear, and finding out how to use effective learning processes (a branch) may be more urgent than delving into a root. On the other hand, if things are not working as well as expected, then it may be important to think more deeply about the roots and how they feed the trunk and underpin the effective learning processes described in the branch. By working up and down the tree, the complexity of the meaning of adaptive expertise will develop. Working through these ideas with colleagues is highly recommended because they often provide insights that a person working in isolation cannot discover alone.

For each of the elements in the tree, vignettes illustrate how a teacher-leader, facilitator, or school or district leader might think and act in relation to the element described. The vignettes bring the descriptions to life in real situations. There are five main characters in the vignettes that are introduced here. Please meet Mateo, the teacher-leader; Penny, the new principal; Liam, the literacy coach (external); Fran, the PL facilitator (external); and Sofia, the district superintendent.

M **Mateo** is a mathematics teacher at a large, urban middle school that serves a mainly Spanish-speaking community in a low-income area. He has recently been asked by his principal to become a teacher-leader and lead the mathematics department in the school. He and his ten colleagues are beginning to look at their curriculum and what they are offering their students for next year. Not many students at Mateo's school take advanced math, and overall the students score below the state average in mathematics assessments. Some of the mathematics teachers have trouble with engagement in their classes.

P **Penny** is the new principal of an elementary school that serves a largely African American community. Penny comes from another state and has not worked in an African American community before. She was very successful in her last school, where she was vice-principal, raising achievement results and leading an engaged team of young teachers. This new school has been without a principal for eight months after the last person became ill. There seem to be some issues with school attendance, and the profile of the school on standardized tests suggests that the students are not making adequate annual progress in literacy and mathematics.

L **Liam** is a literacy coach who works for a consortium that provides professional development experiences for elementary school teachers. He works mainly with linguistically and culturally diverse schools in low-income neighborhoods. His group has recently started working in a new way, offering to mentor and support school or district teams to implement cycles of inquiry with teachers. These inquiry cycles are designed to be evidence based and to personalize PL to the needs of the teachers and schools, which should lead to better learning for teachers. Before this change Liam used to run one- or two-day workshops for teachers, focusing on things like reading comprehension, writing improvement, and formative assessment in literacy.

F **Fran** is an external PL facilitator who goes into middle and high schools to work with leaders. Her expertise is in leadership and educational administration, and she helps new principals or leadership teams to develop a vision for their schools and implement it with their staff. She used to be a principal herself. Fran has a very busy schedule, in and out of a number of schools, and has to keep careful records of what she is doing in each setting, but working across a lot of schools gives her real insight into what is working effectively when leading schools.

S **Sofia** is a superintendent of a K–12 district with about 35,000 students. She was previously the superintendent of a smaller district, and before that she was an elementary principal and teacher. She has responsibility for overseeing the PL of her schools' staff and is interested in shifting PL from teachers going out of school to workshops or events toward PL occurring within schools and being more based around classroom practice needs.

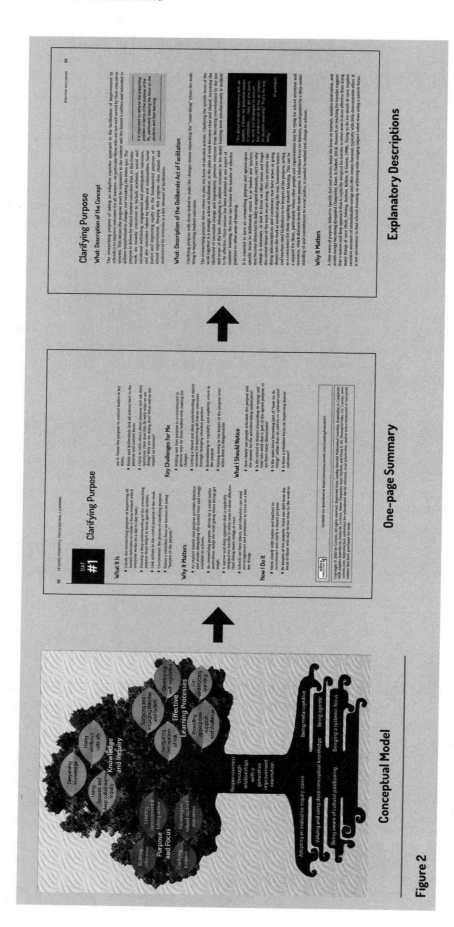

Conceptual Model   **One-page Summary**   **Explanatory Descriptions**

Figure 2

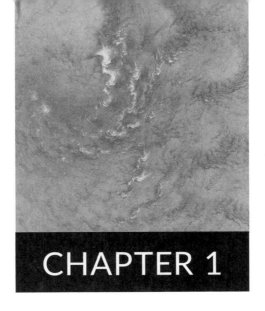

CHAPTER 1

The Roots

Enabling Effective Facilitation

What we do, say, think, and feel in any situation arises from who we are, our dispositions, values, and ways of being. We might know that a certain way of asking questions or a particular technique for giving feedback are useful tools, but if the tools don't mesh with who we are and how we do things we are unlikely to be able to readily and effectively use them. In the tree metaphor we show this by suggesting that some of the characteristics of facilitation with and for adaptive expertise are "roots" of the tree. They are stances, approaches, and ways of being that feed the tree. Without the roots the deliberate acts of facilitation (DAFs) described in Chapter 3 wither and are useless. The roots are essential to give life to the DAFs. Extending the metaphor, the roots also give the tree stability. To do this they form a network of ideas akin to a root system—all the roots are interconnected and necessary to make the tree thrive. The six roots described in this chapter should be seen interdependent, feeding the whole tree. The stronger and deeper the roots, the stronger the tree—and this holds for facilitation with and for adaptive expertise. Strengthening and deepening the elements that ground facilitation practice and provide nourishment to our decisions and interactions will improve our capacity to be responsive and increase our effectiveness as facilitators.

The roots, trunk, branches, and leaves of our metaphorical tree are all part of one organism and are inevitably—and significantly—connected to one another. You will notice that some of the DAFs on the leaves are particularly aligned with certain roots—for example, the use of evidence and focused and deep inquiry as acts of facilitation clearly connect to taking an evaluative inquiry stance toward solving complex problems. All the roots, however, are implicated in each DAF. For example, if we are thinking about using evidence, we need to be very aware of the impact of our cultural positioning, use deep knowledge about types of evidence and how to interpret it, and be metacognitive to monitor our questions and assumptions. Think about these six roots as describing an orientation to facilitating professional learning (PL) that informs, nourishes, and supports any particular action that you might choose to take.

The six roots are as follows:

1. Adopting an evaluative inquiry stance
2. Valuing and using deep conceptual knowledge
3. Being agentic
4. Being aware of cultural positioning

5. Being metacognitive

6. Bringing a systemic focus

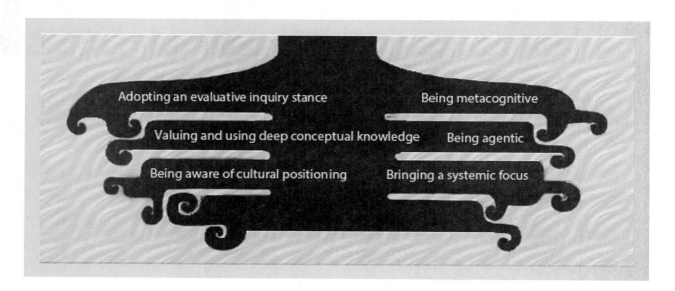

In this chapter each root is presented in a one-page summary, followed by a longer explanation linking the underlying concept from research to the root. This is followed by an explanation of why the root matters, how to "do it," and what some of the key challenges are. The one-page summaries include a brief section on "what to notice" or think about. Each element finishes with two suggestions for further reading and two short vignettes showing what the ideas in the element might look like in practice.

Adopting an Evaluative Inquiry Stance

ROOT #1

What It Is

▶ Have a genuine inquiry and evidence-seeking mindset.

▶ Continually focus on the impact on learners.

▶ Treat own views as ideas that need to be checked.

▶ Be willing to question own and others' beliefs and behavior, and challenge the status quo.

▶ Seek and use evidence and knowledge to inform decision-making.

▶ Be aware that evidence and evaluation are interpretive processes affected by personal biases as well as social and power relationships.

▶ Be open to question own and others' interpretations of evidence.

▶ Engage with different perspectives and the theories and beliefs of others—for example, communities, families, students, leaders, professional colleagues, policy makers.

Why It Matters

▶ An evaluative inquiry stance supports engagement in evidence-informed collaborative inquiry.

▶ There is opportunity to express and test your own views and reasoning while engaging with the views and reasoning of others.

▶ Evaluative inquiry keeps the focus on outcomes for students as the touchstone for change and improvement.

▶ Evaluative inquiry ensures that a range of "narratives" inform decisions and actions rather than privilege a few.

▶ The likelihood of repeating past mistakes and justifying the status quo is reduced.

How I Do It

▶ Ensure information is sought about the impact of our actions

▶ Act on information from others and evidence regarding the impact of our actions

▶ Be tentative about our assumptions and checking them for accuracy before taking further action

▶ Create opportunities for dialogue and collaborative inquiry around choice and timing of deliberate actions

▶ Ensure a focus on problem solving and improvement for the benefit of learners

▶ Ensure work is collaborative and that our joint actions have impact

Key Challenges for Me

▶ "Keeping the main thing the main thing" and avoiding distractions that may not benefit students

▶ Ensuring sufficient time is available for collaborative inquiry

▶ Putting challenging data on the table and being open to a variety of interpretations

▶ Developing, maintaining, and testing our evaluative processes

▶ Being comfortable with ambiguity and disagreement

▶ Being prepared to examine own beliefs and reasoning

▶ Having the skills to identify the most useful forms of evidence

What I Should Notice

▶ What motivates me to be curious? What gets in the way?

▶ Is my curiosity genuine, or do I jump to conclusions and provide solutions?

▶ How do I respond to information that does not align with my own or other peoples' thinking and behavior?

online resources

Available for download at https://resources.corwin.com/LeadingPowerfulPL

Adopting an Evaluative Inquiry Stance

What: Description of the Concept

> *"Collaborative inquiry is a process that recognizes and values teachers as drivers for school improvement, as opposed to being the targets of improvement."*
>
> (Donohoo & Velasco, 2016, p. 4)

Adopting an evaluative inquiry stance requires both the capacity for evaluative thinking (Earl & Timperley, 2016) and bringing an open minded, curious mindset to the work. When these two things are combined, an evaluative inquiry stance ensures that a systematic, open, and reflective process is used. This process involves questioning, using evidence, learning, and developing a warranted argument (Patton, 2011), all the while recognizing our assumptions and blind spots, avoiding jumping to conclusions, and continually checking the validity of what we assume. It is an iterative and dynamic process that contributes to evolving solutions and conclusions.

The phrase "inquiry as stance" was introduced in 2009 by Cochran-Smith and Lytle. In everyday language, stance is used to describe a person's body posture or to describe one's political position. The metaphor of stance was intended by Cochran-Smith and Lytle to capture the concept of the ways we stand, the ways we see, and the lenses we see through. Stance describes our position in relation to something. Sometimes referred to as a "habit of mind" (Earl & Katz, 2006), a stance is a way of being that incorporates dispositional, emotional, motivational, and personality variables. Earl and Katz (2006) explicitly link inquiry to a stance or habit of mind to emphasize that it is a way of thinking that is "a dynamic iterative system to organize ideas, seek out information, and move closer and closer to understanding some phenomenon" (p. 18).

Facilitators can adopt an evaluative inquiry stance approach their work through evaluative thinking. This includes being committed to inquiring into the views and reasoning of others to deepen one's understanding, even when there is disagreement (Robinson, Sinnema, & Le Fevre, 2014); identifying expected outcomes; framing evaluative questions; collecting, interpreting, and using evidence; and sharing insights and findings.

What: Description of the Root

> *"Critical evaluation underscores the need to assess the strengths and weaknesses of the tentative theories . . . produced so as to direct and regulate the evolution of inquiry. It is essential to focus on constructively evaluating the advancement of the inquiry process itself."*
>
> (Katz, Earl, & Jaafar, 2009, p. 72)

Facilitators who adopt an evaluative inquiry stance inquire into the focus and outcomes of their work, particularly in relation to students. They demonstrate a willingness or openness to learning in contrast to being resistant to new ideas. Open-mindedness is more than just being open to other ideas; rather, open-mind edness involves being critically rather than uncritically open to alternative possibilities (Hare, 2006). Being open-minded does not rule out the possibility of holding firm views or advocating them. What it requires is a readiness to reexamine these views in the face of alternative information and new ideas.

Leaders and facilitators need to value deep understanding, be willing to reserve judgment, have a tolerance for ambiguity, have the capacity to take a range of perspectives, and be willing to systematically pose increasingly focused questions (Earl & Katz, 2010). Facilitators with an evaluative inquiry stance are always curious and genuine in wanting to understand what is happening and why. Being willing to engage in genuine inquiry (Le Fevre, Robinson, & Sinnema, 2014) is therefore an essential aspect of an evaluative inquiry stance.

An inquiry stance is dependent on high-quality information, not taken-for-granted assumptions. Evidence and knowledge inform decision-making. At the same time, it is important to be aware that evidence and evaluation are interpretive processes affected by personal biases as well as social and power relationships. Adopting an evaluative inquiry stance requires facilitators to be open to questioning their own and others' interpretations of any evidence and to engage with the theories and beliefs of others.

High-quality evidence refers to both evidence of progress toward improvement and research evidence of what is most likely to be effective in a given situation. This dual use of evidence means that those leading the improvement process both generate evidence related to their own progress (Schildkamp, Lai, & Earl, 2014) and are critical and informed consumers of research evidence.

Why It Matters

Adopting an evaluative inquiry stance matters because data don't make decisions, people do (Datnow, 2011). Evidence-informed inquiry does not simply require good data; it also requires good decisions, and an evaluative inquiry stance enables facilitators to make good decisions in the interests of improving outcomes for students.

> "There is not enough evaluative capability in the school. There is not enough genuine inquiry and urgency about students' achievement."
>
> (Facilitator)

Professional learning communities (PLCs) that undertake collaborative inquiry have been promoted as a way to provide teachers with greater agency and efficacy in making improvements to their practice (Hargreaves & Fullan, 2012). For this to be effective, educators need to be able to focus on valued outcomes for students and to adopt an evaluative inquiry stance. In doing so, they are more likely to analyze what the educational issues are, make good decisions amongst viable options for addressing them, and figure out ways of checking if improvement is being made and sustained.

Engaging people systemically by including communities, families, students, leaders, teachers, professional developers, and policy makers is important if we are to avoid repeating past mistakes and failure to improve, which are all too common scenarios in education (Bryk, Gomez, Grunow, & LeMahieu, 2015). An evaluative inquiry stance welcomes and seeks a range of perspectives to inform initiatives for improvement. In this way a range of "narratives" informs actions rather than just those that justify the status quo or represent the dominant culture.

How I Do It

Effective facilitators continually ask themselves and others the following questions: What evidence is there for this claim? How good is this evidence? And what other evidence or explanations might be considered?

Bringing an evaluative inquiry stance influences the way people interpret and respond to their own and others' actions. This is also a part of seeking information about the impact of one's actions. Not only is it essential to inquire into the impact of our actions but it is also essential to act on this information. This is often the difficult part.

> "The first meeting that we had with the facilitator was with a group of the senior leaders of the school and she asked us some questions, and as we were answering she was asking for evidence straight away."
>
> (Teacher)

Collaborative inquiry is effective when it involves detecting the assumptions that are being made, knowing what questions to ask to check the assumptions, and engaging others in this process (Robinson & Lai, 2006).

As a facilitator, adopting an evaluative inquiry stance involves approaching facilitation with curiosity and an expectation that you will learn from others and creating opportunities for dialogue and collaborative inquiry around choice and timing of deliberate actions.

Key Challenges for Me

Avoiding distractions and "keeping the main thing the main thing" can be a challenge for effective facilitation. It is easy to get distracted by unrelated problems that are part of all educators' daily lives. The main thing is to be focused on improving teaching and leadership practice and relationships with families and communities in ways that have a positive impact on student learning.

To adopt an evaluative inquiry stance that has the capacity to enable improvement, it is important to ensure that time is available for inquiry. Although time may be necessary, it is not sufficient. For example, putting challenging data on the table can be difficult, and the time can be well spent by focusing on what is going on for learners and how to improve their learning environments. Alternatively, time can be wasted by focusing on factors beyond the control of the participants.

Inquiry is difficult work. It can be tempting to jump quickly to solutions and try to get on with problem solving and action quickly. However, in adopting an evaluative inquiry stance there is a commitment to really trying to understand what is happening and how best to address problems of practice. It is very difficult to improve our own practice by reflecting on it in isolation. The assumptions that guide our practice will tend to shape our analyses and evaluations (Robinson & Lai, 2006). Testing our evaluative process can therefore be challenging. In addition there is a tendency in education toward a culture of *niceness*; thus, the need to analyze data that might challenge the perceptions of others is sometimes avoided. Unfortunately, avoidance is not consistent with making a difference for students.

Inquiring with others has the potential to improve our practice as long as we collaborate with everyone—including those whose thinking is different from ours. It means being prepared to challenge others and ourselves in respectful ways.

What I Should Notice

When thinking about our own stance in terms of capacity for evaluative inquiry, we need to ask ourselves the hard personal questions: What motivates me to be curious? How do I respond to information that does not align with my own or other peoples' thinking and behavior? How do I deal with ambiguity? What do I do with what I learn through evaluative inquiry? How do I check if I am being evaluative?

Further Reading

Earl, L., & Timperley, H. (2016). *Embedding evaluative thinking as an essential component of successful innovation* (Seminar Series 257). Melbourne, Australia: Centre for Strategic Education.

Le Fevre, D. M., Robinson, V. M. J., & Sinnema, C. E. L. (2014). Genuine inquiry: Widely espoused but rarely enacted. *Educational Management Administration and Leadership, 43*, 883–899.

Vignette 1a: Adopting an Evaluative Inquiry Stance

 Mateo and his team are working on a year overview for next year, looking at the order of the topics they will teach and how long each one will last. While they are talking about this they begin to talk about the children's achievement in algebra.

	Thomas: The trouble is that the children don't get the algebra quickly enough. We have to move on too fast. It's because they aren't well enough prepared for it. They've got no idea about it when they come in.
	Elisa: I don't know that they've got no idea, but certainly by the end of Grade 8 they are not where they need to be. It's why so many of them drop math as soon as they can—it's just a mystery to them.
Seeing views as needing to be checked **Recognizing assumptions**	**Mateo:** You know, I'm not sure that I've ever really looked closely at what they know when they come in. I've kind of assumed that they are a bit of a blank slate, but maybe they do know some stuff—or maybe what they know gets in the way of learning our material.
	Thomas: What do we get when they come in? Test scores? What happens to those?
Seeing views as needing to be checked **Focusing on learners** **Checking assumptions**	**Mateo:** I know what we could do. Maybe I could get together the stuff that we get on the new students, and we could have a look at it—look at the patterns, what's in there. It might help us test if some of our assumptions are right. Do they know nothing? I mean, I've got my opinion, but I don't actually know if I'm right or not.

Vignette 1b: Adopting an Evaluative Inquiry Stance

 Penny is working with her kindergarten teachers, looking at the children's transition to school and early progress. Teachers in higher grades blame the kindergarten teachers for not moving the children far enough in their first year at school, meaning they are "behind" all the way through. The kindergarten teachers are feeling angry and defensive.

Questioning own and others' beliefs	**Penny:** So you know we've been looking at how the children are doing at our school and what happens to them as they progress through. Some people think the children struggle because they have a slow start. I've heard you all say that they come in a lot lower than the others realize, and they make lots of progress. Can you tell me about what you mean?
	Kayla: Well, when they're new they'll hardly speak, and they don't even know how to sit and listen. We're lucky if they've got some letters or numbers—even colors they're not good at. That's what we are working with.
Checking assumptions with evidence	**Penny:** What information do we collect about what they can do as they arrive? Do we have some evidence we could look at together?
	Tricia: Well, we've got some things for some students, but that's not really helpful for this because it's little steps we're talking about.
Testing assumptions **Checking views** **Recognizing view is limited**	**Penny:** Good point. I wonder what we could do about that? I think we need some more information to look at together here because we are making some assumptions—both about the children and our teaching, which I think we need to test out. And we haven't talked much about what the children can do; maybe there are some things we aren't seeing.
	Kayla: We haven't got time to test all the children again . . .
	Penny: Maybe we could choose some target children to look at closely, get a feel for their experiences.

ROOT #2

Valuing and Using Deep Conceptual Knowledge

What It Is

- Bring experience, knowledge, and confidence about the content and process of your work.
- Knowingly organize and select from a vast pool of knowledge.
- Position self as a learner.
- Be aware both of what one knows and the gaps.
- Value depth of knowledge in self and others.
- Develop knowledge in others, such as leadership and curriculum knowledge, pedagogical knowledge, and knowledge of change processes.

Why It Matters

- Deep knowledge is crucial to feeling confident and capable to deliberately engage in facilitation.
- Deep knowledge permits flexible and responsive work in complex and uncertain settings.
- Leaders value the knowledge and possibilities for practice that facilitators bring to their schools: "images of the possible."
- Decision-making is improved by the use of deep knowledge.

How I Do It

- Be curious and want to explore the worldviews and understandings of others.

- Tap into the "funds of knowledge" within school communities.
- Work from a strengths-based model.
- Value knowledge and evidence from research.
- Begin with what people know and can do.
- Bring and share deep knowledge, theories, and research when working with others.
- Use knowledge to challenge and interrupt problematic beliefs, assumptions, and misconceptions.

Key Challenges for Me

- Being aware of and addressing the gaps in own and others' knowledge
- Moving away from assuming your own knowledge is good enough
- Being prepared to say I don't know

What I Should Notice

- What knowledge do I have?
- What are my needs as a learner and my learners' needs?
- Do I have the knowledge I need to meet others' learning needs?
- What sources are available, and where do I go to develop deep knowledge?

online resources

Available for download at https://resources.corwin.com/LeadingPowerfulPL

Valuing and Using Deep Conceptual Knowledge

What: Description of the Concept

The research literature on learning and transfer clearly establishes the importance of deep conceptual knowledge. It is essential to leadership and facilitation work because it allows people to be adaptive and responsive in every context in which they work. Evidence shows that experts in any field draw on deep conceptual knowledge, which enables them to plan and to notice patterns in what they do. A distinguishable difference between experts and novices is that experts hold a deep understanding of concepts that influence how they interpret and understand new information and novel situations in efficient and effective ways that are not available to novices (Bransford, Brown, & Cocking, 2000). Professional knowledge accumulates over time and becomes part of one's "knowledge base" for practice.

What: Description of the Root

Valuing and using deep conceptual knowledge is fundamental and involves bringing experience, knowledge, and confidence about both the content and process of work to the PL setting. It involves valuing one's own knowledge, the knowledge of others, and the knowledge that might be regarded as formal or research- or evidence-based knowledge. A part of this "valuing" is an ever present intention to deepen understanding and knowledge. The use of conceptual frameworks to enhance understanding enables people to organize and knowingly select from a vast pool of knowledge about leadership and curriculum, pedagogy, and theories of change for improvement as well as content knowledge in the domains of literacy, numeracy, science, the arts, and other subject areas.

> *Deep conceptual knowledge permits flexible and responsive work in complex and uncertain settings.*
> *Deep knowledge is essential to being responsive to the specific needs of learners.*

Valuing and using deep conceptual knowledge involves positioning oneself as a learner as well as being aware both of what we know and what our gaps are. Alongside this awareness of the extent or limit of our own knowledge sits a deep sense of the value of the breadth of our own and others' knowledge. Developing the knowledge of others using conceptual frameworks is fundamental to valuing and using deep conceptual knowledge.

Why It Matters

It is clear from the research into how people learn that deep knowledge is transferable knowledge. It is this ability to access and retrieve relevant knowledge in the PL context that is crucial to feeling confident and capable as a facilitator and leader. Expecting and promoting conceptual coherence also promotes transfer.

Deep knowledge allows people to work flexibly and responsively in complex and challenging settings. Leaders value the knowledge and possibilities for practice that we bring to their schools: our deep conceptual knowledge of change processes and theories of improvement enables stakeholders to perceive images of the possible, or practices and outcomes that are beyond the scope of what is currently happening in the context.

> *"The product of deeper learning is transferable knowledge, including content knowledge in a domain and knowledge of how, why, and when to apply this knowledge to answer questions and solve problems."*
>
> (Pellegrino & Hilton, 2012, pp. 4–5)

The use of deep knowledge also facilitates improved decision-making by providing a wealth of information from experience and theory. Deep knowledge allows us to readily perceive important connections and useful synergies.

How I Do It

> "I did have my knowledge there so that I didn't have to go looking for it . . . Everything I do files into my head and I constantly use this as I decide on the move that I will make next . . . back."
>
> (Facilitator)

We can value and use deep conceptual knowledge in our work by bringing and sharing knowledge, theories, and research when working with others. We can use our knowledge to challenge and interrupt problematic beliefs, assumptions, and misconceptions, which is necessary before leaders and teachers can engage in new learning themselves. Being curious and wanting to explore the worldviews and understandings of others promotes an environment in which new knowledge is valued and sought.

Beginning from a strengths-based model with what people know and can do and tapping into the funds of knowledge within school communities facilitates the acquisition of new knowledge. It is also important to link new learning to existing knowledge through the use of conceptual frameworks. An effective and responsive way to access and share the depth and breadth of knowledge within a school community is through encouraging the telling of stories and the use of metaphor. Both storytelling and metaphor are powerful ways of making sense of experiences.

Key Challenges for Me

> "You might have knowledge . . . but I don't think I've got enough knowledge. Finding out from someone else and seeking new knowledge is important."
>
> (Facilitator)

Being aware of and addressing the gaps in our own and others' knowledge is an ongoing challenge in PL work. As new situations arise, it is important to continue to assess the available and the missing knowledge required to meet the needs of the improvement challenge; it is important to constantly be aware of what knowledge is needed in the moment. It can also be difficult to say I don't know, particularly in a situation where one feels an expectation to be the "expert."

What I Should Notice

It is important to begin from a strengths-based perspective by discovering what knowledge people already have and to effectively diagnose what their learning needs are within the context of the PL. It is also essential to identify whether or not we have the knowledge we need to meet others' learning needs and to identify the sources that are available to develop the requisite deep knowledge in others and ourselves. Keep asking yourself this: How does this fit in with what I believe and know about facilitating improvement in schools, and what do I need to learn to be an effective facilitator or leader in this context?

Further Reading

Bransford, J., Brown, A., & Cocking, R. (2000). *How people learn: Brain, mind, experience and school.* Washington DC: National Academies Press.

Pellegrino, J., & Hilton, M. (Eds.). (2012). *Education for life and work: Developing transferable knowledge and skills in the 21st century.* Washington, DC: National Academies Press.

Vignette 2a: Valuing and Using Deep Conceptual Knowledge

 Penny is worried about school attendance. She has been looking at the attendance data and there are lots of children who attend very erratically; therefore, she feels that the parents aren't committed to sending the children to school. She is chatting to a teacher who is a local community member and has been at the school for a long time about her concerns.

	Penny: It just seems like the parents here don't value their children's education. Here we are, right in the center of the community, ready to serve, and they don't even make the effort to get their children here each day.
Being curious about the worldviews of others	**Barbara:** It's a bit different from where you came from? **Penny:** Yeah, there we had parents banging down the door, demanding more homework, more events, more communication. Here it feels like they don't even care. You know, actually, I don't know how they feel when I think about it. I'm assuming it means they don't care, but I don't know. I wonder how they do feel?
	Barbara: I think that's the question to ask: How do the parents and community see the school?
Tapping into funds of knowledge	**Penny:** You know, I've kind of come in here and been so busy getting started that I've never really asked that question, about how the school sits in the community, what it means to them . . .
	Barbara: There've been ups and downs with it, that's for sure. Remember not all the parents had success at school like we did. I'm sure we could learn a lot from them if we asked.
Valuing others' knowledge	**Penny:** Tell me some more about that? How could we go about doing it?

Vignette 2b: Valuing and Using Deep Conceptual Knowledge

L Liam is working with elementary school literacy leaders from several schools in one district. They are talking about children with home languages other than English and their progress in English literacy.

	Melissa: So we just can't get them started on English really. They don't speak up in class, they don't practice at home, they seem stuck. I don't know how much they are going to learn from just being there.
	Carlos: Yeah, I'm okay with the Spanish-speaking kids because I speak Spanish, so we can get around it for content learning, but it's not building their English and for the others—well, I know some stuff, but it just isn't working.
Bringing experience, knowledge, and confidence about the content and process of your work	**Liam:** I wonder what their literacy is like in their first language. Bilingual learning pathways are different from monolingual learning pathways, but the outcomes can be really powerful if we know how to encourage and teach them. There are some frameworks and research findings on this that we could look at as a group to help us.
	Melissa: I really feel like they don't know anything much, either way.
Interrupting problematic assumptions	**Liam:** I think we need to explore that assumption because that could undermine what we do. Research suggests that they have knowledge that schools are not very good at noticing or using, but if we can find ways to use it, we can work with them to improve their literacy—in both languages.
	Carlos: I'd be interested to know what that means in practice—like what should we do day to day?

ROOT #3 Being Agentic

What It Is

- Have a strong sense of personal efficacy.
- Recognize that agency is both a personal quality within educators and is mediated by interaction with the context (e.g., cultural, structural, power, relationships).
- Recognize that agency is influenced by past experience, engagement in the present, and vision of the future.
- Respond innovatively and persistently to promote equity and improvement.
- Have a strong sense of social justice and moral purpose that all learners can learn "no matter what."

Why It Matters

- Being agentic is fundamental for improving equity.
- There are many obstacles to overcome and agency underpins persistence.
- Agency enables power and control to be used in ways that benefit learners.
- Collective efficacy and agency are needed to increase impact and create sustainable change.
- Active involvement of others (e.g., learners and their families) increases collective efficacy.

How I Do It

- Be prepared to persist and innovate even when it becomes difficult.
- Support and challenge others to be agentic in their theorizing about learners.
- Express personal commitment and responsibility for every learner.
- Explicitly reject own and others' deficit theorizing about learners and their families and educators.
- Use a strengths-based collaborative approach to learning.
- Develop agency in others in order to build collective agency within the organization.

Key Challenges for Me

- Focusing on long-term visions or goals rather than quick fixes
- Committing to take action against deficit beliefs
- Dealing with low morale and "chaotic" contexts
- Challenging actions that reinforce negative stereotypes and biases

What I Should Notice

- Do I believe that leaders and teachers here can make a difference?
- Are my narratives reinforcing deficit theorizing about leaders, teachers, and students, or are they promoting agency in talking about learners?
- Am I supporting leaders and teachers to develop their agency and change how they practice?
- Do I encourage leaders and teachers to share notions of social justice rather than blame learners?

online resources ⌖ Available for download at https://resources.corwin.com/LeadingPowerfulPL

Being Agentic

What: Description of the Concept

Having a sense of agency both individually and collectively is foundational to adaptive expertise. At a broad level, agency is about our ability to intentionally influence circumstances in life. Having agency allows us to influence our own and others' experiences and the environment, rather than merely reacting to experience. Agency can be personal, proxy, or collective. Personal agency is individually driven while proxy agency relies on the actions of others to get things done. Collective agency happens through the coordinated and interdependent actions of a group or groups (Bandura, 2001).

> A central concept in agency is self-efficacy or the "belief that one has the power to produce desired effects by one's actions."
>
> (Bandura, 2001, p. 270)

Agency has typically been viewed as a personal quality within people; however, more recently it has come to be recognized as mediated by the dynamic interaction of the person(s) with their context. Agency is influenced by our past experiences, the present situation, and our vision for the future (Biesta, Priestly, & Robinson, 2015). This means that it is possible to have our agency affected by past experiences and to feel different levels of agency, such as agency in one setting but not another. An example of this may be that we feel we have agency in one specific classroom; however, in a setting that we are not familiar with, or that is highly prescriptive, we may feel our ability to act as an agent of change is compromised or reduced.

A central concept underpinning agency is self-efficacy, or the belief that we have the power to gain the results or effect needed through our actions (Bandura, 2001). Importantly, this includes having the self-efficacy needed to motivate others when working as a facilitator. Collective efficacy is an important component of collective agency where members hold "shared beliefs in the power to produce desired effects by collective action" (Bandura, 2001, p. 271). Without these beliefs that the person and or the group can make a difference, there is little motivation to act. Collective teacher efficacy, or the "perception and judgments of a group of educators regarding their ability to positively influence student outcomes" (Donohoo, 2017, p. 102), is ranked the number one influence on student achievement (Donohoo, Hattie, & Eells, 2018), emphasizing the power of agentic beliefs to make a difference.

Intentionality, forethought, and self-regulation are important aspects of agency. Intentionality is about using one's power to take planned action so that outcomes are the consequence of deliberate planned actions. Forethought refers to considering future outcomes in relation to what is happening now. Self-regulation as part of agency includes how we shape, motivate, and monitor our actions along with metacognitive reflection on our motivations, values, and goals. Moral purpose or moral agency (Bandura, 2001) is also an important part of making decisions and doing the "right thing." This agency can be of an inhibitive nature (e.g., not acting badly) or proactive, where one takes positive action.

What: Description of the Root

Research has focused on the notion of "being agentic" or taking an agentic position in response to long-standing educational disparities for New Zealand's indigenous students. Bishop and his colleagues revealed the importance of educators bringing a strong sense of moral purpose or moral agency to promote equity in their classrooms for indigenous Maori students. Being agentic is about educators "being able to express their professional commitment and responsibility to bringing about change in . . . educational achievement and accept professional responsibility for the learning of their students" (Bishop, 2010, p. 61). In practice this means not only proactively taking a positive and strengths-based position when we theorize about students, their achievement, and their families but also actively rejecting the deficit theories that prevail in many schools about the achievement of groups of students, such as indigenous students, minority students, and those with special educational needs.

> *"Despite our being well-meaning, with the best intentions in the world, if students with whom we are interacting as teachers are led to believe that we think they are deficient, they will respond to this negatively."*
>
> (Bishop, 2010, p. 58)

Being agentic underpins our drive to make change for those currently underserved by schools and educational systems. This includes holding a strong belief that using pedagogies that honor cultural and linguistic diversity will make a difference for learners. Being agentic is important as a facilitator because change requires a belief that we can make a difference to a situation despite the odds and underpins having the courage to try new ways of working to achieve more equitable outcomes. It also involves promoting others to develop agency and belief at the collective level. Collective agency means that power and control are shared among the people who can respond to student learning needs at all levels of the organization.

Agency and self-efficacy are similar concepts and often used interchangeably. As a root, being agentic is driven by one's self-efficacy beliefs to make a difference but also includes having the courage to intentionally take the necessary action to influence outcomes. This demands relentlessly challenging the status quo and proactively taking a social justice stance even when this is uncomfortable and may feel impossible. Improvement can happen when we do.

Why It Matters

To be effective, educators need to believe their intentional actions can have a positive impact on educational settings and that they have the capacity to make a difference for learners—especially for learners who have traditionally been underserved by the system. Agency is central to the well-being of young people and adults alike. Facilitators have the important dual role of being agentic and developing collective agency with others. Being agentic means having a strong sense that we can make a difference and holding the belief that we can act to improve valued educational outcomes for students when working in a variety of contexts and addressing a range of educational problems. It also matters because, if we are agentic as facilitators, we will be more able to support others to be agentic and not only believe but also take action to make a difference for students. To make a difference we have to take intentional action to improve equity in student outcomes and check whether we actually have made that difference.

How I Do It

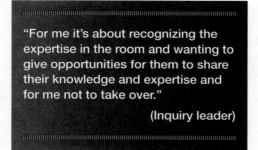

> "For me it's about recognizing the expertise in the room and wanting to give opportunities for them to share their knowledge and expertise and for me not to take over."
>
> (Inquiry leader)

Being agentic influences the decisions and actions an educator takes. We demonstrate being agentic when we believe we can make a difference for all our students and deliberately express our personal commitment and responsibility for each learner. This means we are prepared to persist with innovative actions even when it gets difficult or seems against the odds.

It is important that we explicitly and openly reject our own deficit theorizing about leaders, teachers, learners, and their families. We need to see others and ourselves as being capable and able to make positive change. Being agentic is also about making deliberate choices to challenge and prevent problematic practices. When we use a strengths-based approach in our work, we communicate to others that we believe that all learners can learn and that self-efficacy and agency can be built through positive engagement in learning. Helping others to take a strengths-based approach to their roles builds these understandings in others too.

Collective agency or efficacy is necessary for successful change (Donohoo, 2016; Donohoo et al., 2018); we can't do it on our own. It is essential that we deliberately develop agency and self-efficacy beliefs in others in order to build collective agency within the organization in which we are working.

Key Challenges for Me

One of the key challenges in being agentic is being prepared to take action against negative and deficit thinking. Using a sense of moral agency in order to make a difference can be uncomfortable and very challenging when it involves questioning deeply held beliefs, and actions of others—especially culture-based beliefs and bias that reinforce low expectations of diverse learners. It can be easier to ignore and maintain the status quo; however, by not taking action, there will be little or no change for these learners.

> "You think you are opening up conversations, but I'm not sure what worms I'm letting out of the can. The issue is if I let them out of the can, am I able to then use them constructively—I need to feel able to work with what I let out."
>
> (Facilitator)

As educators, we need to focus on the future long-term vision rather than quick fixes, even when it gets hard, such as in contexts where there is low morale or even chaos. At other times, difficult past and current experiences may necessitate additional intentionality or support to continue to be agentic. This is when our personal self-efficacy and moral purpose are paramount.

What I Should Notice

The ideal context to work toward is one where there is collective efficacy and agency. It is important to check our own beliefs about whether we can make a difference as well as whether leaders and teachers believe they can make a difference and how they theorize about each other, students, and their families. Do our narratives inadvertently reinforce deficit theorizing about leaders, teachers, students, or families rather than promoting notions of social justice and agency in talking about learners? Do we work toward building others' agency when we work together to change practices or are we encouraging reliance on external support? Do we self-regulate and check how much of a difference we are making?

Further Reading

Bishop, R. (2010). Effective teaching for indigenous and minoritized students. *Procedia Social and Behavioral Sciences, 7*, 57–62.

Donohoo, J. (2016). *Collective efficacy: How educators' beliefs impact student learning.* Thousand Oaks, CA: Corwin.

Vignette 3a: Being Agentic

L Liam has found himself in a difficult situation. He is facilitating a discussion with the staff of an elementary school where he hasn't worked before. He was asked to come in and help with some ideas about improving the teaching of writing and started the teachers off with an exercise to identify the students' strengths and weaknesses in writing. He gave them a chart to record these on. The teachers have skipped over strengths and gone straight to weaknesses, revealing an underlying deficit orientation toward learners. They are saying things like the following:

> "These kids won't need to write anyway."
>
> "Their parents and grandparents couldn't write, so I don't know what we expect."
>
> "Do you think there's reading and writing going on at home? I don't think so. The children never see it except at school."
>
> "I'm not sure why we bother teaching them to write. They'll have lost it again by high school."

(Continued)

(Continued)

	"They don't really come from writing cultures. It's not part of who they are."
	Liam doesn't know the staff yet, so he doesn't have a relationship with them, making it hard to tackle these statements without sounding judgmental or superior.
Using own agency to address difficult situations **Being explicit about agency** **Addressing deficit thinking, even when it is hard**	Instead of ignoring it, or letting it go, however, Liam decides to address it. He writes up some statements on the whiteboard that are close to what he has heard (so as not to pinpoint anyone) and reflects back to the teachers that this is what he has heard. He makes it clear that he thinks they can all make a difference for these learners, but that deficit thinking of this sort affects teaching and assessment decisions and will "haunt" their improvement work if they don't tackle it. As a first step he invites the teachers to look at the statements and flip them around: What if the kids really need to learn to write in order to improve their life chances? What would that mean? What if there is reading and writing at home, but we might not be recognizing it? What if there are oral traditions, music, storytelling, and other forms of literacy that could be used to help "school learning"? In this discussion Liam emphasizes the agency that the teachers have and their responsibility to use it in ways that recognize children's strengths and capacities.

Vignette 3b: Being Agentic

 Mateo has decided to look at some student data with his team. He is concerned about some of the things he has heard teachers say about students in the staff room. It seems to be acceptable to have low expectations of the students' mathematics learning, especially for the native Spanish speakers. The teachers say things like this:

Using own agency to address difficult situations	"These kids just don't have mathematical brains. They are too emotional and artsy." "I don't need to worry too much about my eighth graders. They aren't going to keep taking math anyway, so if we skip the harder parts, it's easier on all of us." Mateo hopes to use the data as a "neutral" way to reexamine the students, their strengths, and their learning needs.
Addressing deficit thinking, even when it is hard	*Mateo:* So, I thought we'd have a look at some data together, as we're trying to make decisions about our curriculum and expectations. It seems to me that we need to come back to what our students know and can do. I want to start with one of my classes that is struggling and get you all to help me if that's okay. *Elisa:* Sure, if we can.
	Mateo gives out some graphs on paper, so people can write on them. *Mateo:* I made these graphs, looking at the students' results across all the unit tests we've done this semester. The first one is everyone, but then I split it out into genders and ethnicity and into native and nonnative English speakers. Have a look and see if you can notice any patterns? *Thomas:* Wow, we really need to separate out the English learners into another class. *Mateo:* Let's just start with looking at the data before we think about solutions. What are you noticing?

	Elisa: It looks like the whole class struggled with the geometry work.
	Thomas: You've got some students here who have scored consistently well across all the other topics—though I'm surprised at how well they've done.
	Elisa: I'm not seeing a big difference among genders, but language seems to be a big factor.
Expressing commitment and professional responsibility	*Mateo:* Yeah, I'm concerned about that. I need to do something different in my teaching, I think—make it more accessible. I can use two languages—which helps some of them—but there's something about the way I'm teaching that's not getting through, even to the Spanish speakers. I'm worried about them not understanding me in either language! *Thomas:* I find they just don't want to concentrate. They drift off.
Being explicit about agency	*Mateo:* It can seem like that, but I think that probably has something to do with the way I'm teaching it. I'm thinking about trying a more contextualized approach and having the students in groups. I want to see if I can get more dialogue going. I think I can engage them more with the math concepts that way. Has anyone had any success using group activities?

ROOT #4

Being Aware of Cultural Positioning

What It Is

- View linguistic and cultural responsiveness (LCR) as a way of being and working, not an add-on.
- Hold a deep personal commitment to social justice.
- Value diversity in learning and learners.
- Demonstrate a willingness to question own and others' assumptions.
- Have a desire to create strong, trusting, and respectful relationships.
- Be aware of the privileged nature of some knowledge and the negative effects of this.

Why It Matters

- Identity, culture, and language play a central role in learning at all levels.
- Cultural positioning influences what we notice, ignore, and act on.
- Commitment to LCR action is critical to improving educational outcomes for diverse learners.
- LCR is often espoused but not enacted.
- Learners are empowered or disempowered as a result of interactions in school.
- Knowledge building about LCR practice is critical for change.

How I Do It

- Create commitment to diverse students' success.
- Value family and community knowledge so that success includes, not excludes, students' culture, language, and identities.
- Co-construct commitment to action with educators, families, and community knowledge holders.
- Take a strengths-based approach to engaging others in taking action.
- Develop relationships of respect.
- Make language and culture central to learning and teaching programmed.

Key Challenges for Me

- Recognizing potential discomfort in cultural biases and confronting assumptions
- Embedding languages and culture across school practices and within teaching and learning programs
- Existing priorities and creating space for community knowledge within curriculum planning and programs
- Developing equitable reciprocal relationships for learning

What I Should Notice

- What are my narratives, stories, or metaphors?
- What are my own (sometimes "invisible") cultural biases?
- What are the effects of my power?
- What do I notice, and what untapped potential might I be ignoring?

 online resources   Available for download at https://resources.corwin.com/LeadingPowerfulPL

Being Aware of Cultural Positioning

What: Description of the Concept

Cultural positioning is about the way people experience the world through specific cultural lenses. These cultural lenses are affected by the communities people grow up in and the expectations of families and others whom they interact with on a regular basis. When people are aware of their own cultural positioning they can become aware of the possible impact of cultural biases and ways of thinking on their actions. Publicly acknowledging our own cultural positioning as a leader or facilitator can enable others to become more aware of how they are culturally positioned. Being consciously aware of our own culture enables us to notice the cultures of the students in our classrooms. A key aspect of understanding our cultural positioning as a leader of learning is questioning our own assumptions and working to understand the position, experiences, and views of others.

What: Description of the Root

Being aware of our own and others' cultural positioning involves viewing LCR as a way of being and working, not as an add-on. It does not comprise a discrete set of actions but rather imbues and influences all aspects of our practice. It is an integral part of holding a deep, personal commitment to social justice, because it requires us to acknowledge the profound inequities in societies worldwide that have been promoted and perpetuated by the historical privileging of certain cultures—usually the dominant white culture—over others.

> *"The culture of the child cannot enter the classroom until the teacher is consciously aware of it."*
>
> (McKenzie & Singleton, 2009)

Being aware of our own cultural positioning allows us to value diversity in learning and learners. One of the identified causes of disparity in achievement among different ethnic and cultural groups in education systems involves historical precedents of valuing certain kinds of knowledge and ways of learning over others, and it is important that we facilitate the vital shift toward education systems that values and promotes diverse and culturally identified ways of knowing and learning. We participate in this shift by acknowledging and valuing other cultures but also by recognizing, valuing, and being prepared to share our own.

An important part of dismantling the entrenched hierarchies around valued knowledge and ways of learning in our schools is demonstrating a willingness to question our own and others' assumptions. Often the cultural biases in our own and others' practices are unconscious (Blank, Houkamau, & Kingi, 2016), and these can be "invisible." Being aware and up front about our own cultural positioning is the first step on the journey to uncovering and addressing those possibly deep-seated and entrenched biases. Being aware of the privileged nature of some knowledge—and the negative effects of this for all learners—is essential.

A desire to create strong, trusting, and respectful relationships with those with whom we work in schools and in other parts of our work motivates us to be open about our own cultural positioning and to acknowledge and value the cultural positioning of others. It is impossible to be responsive to the cultures of others if we don't first consider our own.

> "I didn't have the language. I didn't have the framework. I was hung up by what I had previously experienced in my work and what I could bring to it. I guess it's what some of the students experience all the time."
>
> (Facilitator)

Why It Matters

It is important to be aware of our own and other's cultural positioning because identity, culture, and language play a central role

> *A key aspect of understanding one's cultural positioning as a facilitator is questioning one's own assumptions and working to understand the position, experiences, and views of others.*

in learning at all levels. International research has established the profound importance of the individual's cultural and linguistic identity in their educational success as well as the corresponding lack of achievement when learners' cultures and languages are discounted within or excluded from educational settings. School failure has lifelong negative consequences for the person and society (Organisation for Economic Co-operation and Development [OECD], 2012).

A commitment to linguistically and culturally responsive action is critical to improving educational outcomes for diverse learners, but this way of working is often espoused but not enacted. The culture and language of diverse learners is often only acknowledged and addressed in schools in superficial and token ways, because educational leaders and teachers have not first examined and come to grips with their own cultural positioning in relation to the cultures of their learners. As facilitators, we can set a crucial example in the way we are up front about who we are and what we bring to our work from a cultural and linguistic point of view.

Our cultural positioning influences what we notice and act on, which means firstly that we must be explicit about our own cultural positioning in order to notice and act in responsive ways in our work and secondly that we must encourage leaders and teachers in schools to be similarly aware of their own cultural positioning in order that they might also notice and act responsively. When the culture of the child enters the consciousness of educators, we must also examine our own frames of reference to ensure that we don't judge others against our own "normal." Then we can acknowledge the equity traps such as deficit thinking that can "ensnare, undermine, and defeat the ability of educators to create equitable schools" (McKenzie & Scheurich, 2004, p. 628).

How I Do It

Being aware of our own and others' cultural positioning means we are committed and create commitment in others to linguistically and culturally diverse students' success. We seek out and value family and community knowledge so that success is built on students' cultural identities, rather than denying or ignoring them. We co-construct commitment to action with teachers, leaders, and community knowledge holders. We also take a strengths-based approach to engaging others in taking action. We develop relationships of respect built on mutual trust and openness about our cultural positioning as well as ensure that language and culture are central to learning and teaching programmed.

Key Challenges for Me

There are many challenges in being aware of our own and others' cultural positioning. Many of the participants in our research into the facilitation of LCR acknowledged their high perceptions of risk and feelings of vulnerability in engaging in the research. There is a great deal of potential discomfort in recognizing cultural biases and confronting assumptions, particularly when we identify with the dominant culture. We can feel responsible for perpetuating social and educational inequities.

> "For me it's been challenging—it's been thinking about being a bit more upfront about that as opposed to . . . being as blended as I possibly can; it's being more upfront about who I am and what I bring to the table. And so that gives everybody an opportunity to share who they are and what they bring to the table."
>
> (Facilitator)

Once we have surfaced and challenged our own and others' assumptions about culturally and linguistically diverse learners and ways of knowing and learning, it is enormously challenging to embed languages and culture across school practices and within teaching and learning programs. Prioritizing and creating space for community knowledge within curriculum planning is an important part of this process but may be viewed by some stakeholders as superfluous or unnecessarily complicated and time consuming unless we successfully model the importance of being aware of our own and others' cultural positioning.

Developing equitable reciprocal relationships for learning can be challenging because of perceived power relationships among staff in schools and also between external "experts" and school staff. These relationships can become more difficult because of the high levels of perceived risk and vulnerability involved in being open about our own cultural identity, particularly in relation to others of different cultures. The importance of mutual trust and respect in relationships is particularly salient here.

What I Should Notice

When considering the question of how we become aware of our own and others' cultural positioning within our facilitation work and how we place this acknowledgment of our culture at the heart of our professional identity, we can begin by asking ourselves what narratives, stories, and metaphors have value to us in our lives and work. These help us to understand our own cultural positioning and offer us a way of sharing our culture with others.

We also need to pay close attention to our own cultural biases. These are likely to be deep seated and may be unacknowledged or invisible to us, so we need to be particularly receptive to the dissonance that occurs when we encounter someone whose point of view differs from ours and to be ready to ask ourselves the difficult questions. We need to be prepared to consider and acknowledge the effects of our power and its impact on our relationships with others—particularly in relation to our cultural positioning. We must also ask what haven't we seen because of our cultural positioning and look for the untapped potential in our diverse learners.

Further Reading

Organisation for Economic Co-operation and Development. (2012). *Equity and quality in education: Supporting disadvantaged students and schools*. Paris, France: OECD Publishing. Retrieved from http://dx.doi.org/10.1787/9789264130852-en

Sleeter, C. E. (2001). Preparing teachers for culturally diverse schools: Research and the overwhelming presence of whiteness. *Journal of Teacher Education, 52*, 94–106.

Vignette 4a: Being Aware of Cultural Positioning

P Penny is talking to her vice-principal about holding a parent night to let the parents know about the teacher inquiry into reading that the school is starting.

Questioning assumptions Understanding that cultural biases can be invisible	*Penny:* I started out thinking we would model the evening on what we did at my last school. It was really successful. We did a straight-after-work thing to catch people before they went home, had some food and entertainment for the kids, gave the parents a drink and some nice nibbles. Lots of people came. But after what we've been talking about and you helping me understand this community and ways we might connect school and home, I'm wondering if that's the right approach.
	David: Yeah. What works well in one place might not work so well in another. But we've never been very successful at getting parents to come to school events for them. They turn out to see their kids though. They love watching them perform or play sports.

(Continued)

(Continued)

| Desiring to create trusting and respectful relationships

Questioning assumptions

Being aware of the privileged nature of some knowledge	*Penny:* When I was talking to the local pastor last week, he was speaking about some of the things they do at the church—and a bit about why they do things that way. I think I need to question some of my assumptions about the whole thing—I mean, first of all, we've been talking about getting to know the community and their aspirations better, but I've been planning a one-way, us-to-them dialogue for this meeting. Maybe there are other ways to get the information out there. Actually, we need a way to hear their ideas and knowledge too—two-way flow. Are meetings even the best thing?
Being aware of the privileged nature of some knowledge

Understanding that cultural biases can be invisible | *David:* You're right. It's so easy to slip into thinking from what we want to achieve—and at the moment we are thinking that our knowledge is what needs to be shared. It's probably not the best way to build relationships. |
| Demonstrating willingness to question assumptions | *Penny:* Okay. Well, let's start a new way then. How about we ask a group of parents who come to school often and already know us. Maybe they would be willing to meet and have a chat about options or ideas. We could plan for the evening together. |

Vignette 4b: Being Aware of Cultural Positioning

S Sofia is planning to meet with all her principals over a two-day retreat to talk about the vision for their district and where they are going together. She has invited some principals to join her to work out how the retreat will run.

| Questioning assumptions

Understanding that cultural biases can be invisible	*Sofia:* Thanks for coming. I think this retreat will be really important for us—a time to get together and thrash out where we are going and what we really stand for and also to start that long process of aligning what we are doing with what we believe. But I need your help. I'm really aware that as the superintendent of the organization—and who I am and where I come from—that I can see things differently to others. So I'm hoping we can do this together. How does that sound?
	Brian: Nice to be asked, happy to part of it.
Desiring to create trusting and respectful relationships

Valuing diversity | *Joanne:* I think how we meet, the process and protocols, is going to be really important for making it safe for everyone to contribute. I'm not just talking about this group. The diversity of our schools is not really represented in our principals. We need to honor our district by working in ways that include everyone. |
Valuing diversity	*Sofia:* Absolutely. So that means we are going to have to work out who we need to include in our visioning—and how we ensure we can get all the different voices heard. One of the things I've been thinking about is the linguistic diversity that's present in our district. I'd like to see that given more prominence when we meet, making it clear it's a strength and not a problem.
	José: We talk a lot about social justice, but I think we need to dig into what that means, what it looks like—not just hand on heart stuff. What are we doing? And how do we make sure we embed it in our vision?
Having a deep commitment to social justice	*Sofia:* We also need to make our resourcing, especially PL follow our values and purpose, so what would a PL plan that values social justice be like? That might be interesting to talk about. We've got a lot to consider. Let's start by working on how we will go about the visioning process.

Being Metacognitive

What It Is

- Be aware of own thinking, reasoning, and feelings.
- Explain own thinking, reasoning, and feelings to others, and encourage others to explain their thinking, reasoning, and feelings.
- Have a continual awareness of any possible consequences (cognitive and affective) on others' decisions.
- Understand strategies for planning, analyzing, and increasing knowledge.
- Check in and respond to possible consequences of own actions on other people.

Why It Matters

- Metacognition enables deliberate action.
- Metacognition creates understanding of what is driving own and others' actions and influencing feelings.
- Responsiveness is enabled through constant awareness of situation for others.
- Ongoing reflection is central and paramount to decision-making.

How I Do It

- Continually seek to understand how others are thinking about their thinking.
- Uncover people's reasoning.
- Make visible different ways of interpreting events.
- Prompt continual questioning and metacognitive engagement in examining what is happening.

Key Challenges for Me

- Considering multiple perspectives at once
- Making decisions based on multiple perspectives
- Being metacognitive when the going gets tough and there is a tendency to just act

What I Should Notice

- What am I communicating when I "think aloud"?
- How do I react to others thinking aloud?
- What do I do when people have different views?

Being Metacognitive

What: Description of the Concept

> *"Metacognition has been defined as knowledge about cognition and control of cognition."*
>
> (Flavell, 1979)

Metacognition has been defined as knowledge about cognition and control of cognition (Bransford et al., 2000). When a person is metacognitive (also called having metacognitive awareness) they are aware of the way they use what they know about themselves and others as learners. A part of being metacognitive is using metacognitive knowledge. This is knowledge about our cognitive and learning processes and includes understanding our strategies for planning, analyzing, and gaining more knowledge. In essence, being metacognitive involves thinking about our thinking.

The other part of being metacognitive is self-regulation (sometimes referred to as metacognitive control or metacognitive regulation). This is the regulation of cognition and learning experiences through a set of activities that help people control their learning (Flavell, 1979). In facilitation work this might look like, for example, intentionally analyzing learning situations, creating plans and goals, monitoring and modifying plans, being aware of negative emotions, and evaluating overall outcomes.

The two key components of metacognition (metacognitive knowledge and self-regulation) interact in a dynamic way in learning (Bransford et al., 2000).

Facilitators have the important role of increasing their own and others' capability in being metacognitive. Being metacognitive demands that facilitators are both aware of their own thinking and reasoning and are able to explain their thinking and reasoning to others. In addition, supporting others to be metacognitive involves helping others to do this and to actively monitor their own learning.

The concept of metacognition is often thought about in terms of having an awareness and regulation of cognition or thinking. Another important aspect of metacognition is having awareness of how feelings influence how we think and act. The affective aspect of learning is recognized as central to learning (Boekaerts, 2010), and metacognition includes being aware of our emotional responses and the impact these may have on our actions. Learning will occur best when prior knowledge and beliefs are engaged, when deep knowledge is built on conceptual frameworks, and when metacognition and self-regulation are promoted (Bransford et al., 2000).

What: Description of the Root

The personal quality or disposition of being metacognitive is central to adaptive expertise. Being metacognitive demands both being metacognitive oneself as a leader and facilitator while at the same time developing metacognition in those with whom one works.

High levels of metacognition for oneself as a leader or facilitator are a necessary part of leading or facilitating effective PL. Being metacognitive means facilitators are aware of the beliefs and theories that drive their decision-making; in other words they are thinking about their own thinking.

Effective facilitators are continually self-aware and reflecting on both the content and process of their facilitation. This includes having a continual awareness of the possible cognitive and affective consequences for others of any decisions made. An example of a process that demands one to be deeply metacognitive is engaging in the spiral of inquiry (Timperley, Kaser, & Halbert, 2014). The spiral of inquiry guides educators through the metacognitive work of understanding how they can know what is happening for learners. Metacognition enables educators to make informed decisions that improve learning through seeking and using evidence about learning and checking assumptions.

In the past, metacognition has tended to focus primarily on cognitive processes and knowledge acquisition, on how people are thinking about things. However, more recent research has highlighted the importance of focusing on how people are feeling and what their emotional responses are. Emotion and motivation are considered "gatekeepers of learning" (Dumont, Istance, & Benavides, 2012). Facilitators who are metacognitive are aware that it is also very important to be aware of and respond to both their own and others' affective responses in learning.

Developing metacognition in others underpins adaptive expertise in effective facilitation. By being metacognitive oneself, being aware and transparent about the possible intended and unintended consequences of one's actions, facilitators can support those they work with to also be this way. Developing metacognition in others involves encouraging them to share their thinking and reasoning through thinking aloud, reflecting on their own practice and feelings, and questioning each other (Darling-Hammond & Bransford, 2005).

Why It Matters

Being metacognitive enables facilitators to be deliberate in their acts of facilitation. Without metacognition it would actually be very difficult to be deliberate in a meaningful and responsive way. Being metacognitive means that as facilitators we are paying constant attention to what might be driving both our own and others' actions, what is influencing our own and others' thoughts, and, importantly, what the possible causes and consequences are of our own and others' feelings. People who are highly metacognitive "continually self-assess their performances and modify their

> *Being metacognitive enables facilitators to consider the possible causes and consequences of our own and others' feelings. This is important as emotion acts as a "gatekeeper of learning."*

assumptions and actions as needed. People who are less metacognitive rely on external feedback from others to tell them what to do and how to change" (Darling-Hammond & Bransford, 2005, p. 376).

The capacity to be metacognitive is particularly important in the work of improving education as it is used to help people to learn about the cognitive processes that underlie their actions. By thinking about their underlying thinking, people have the possibility to better understand their own and others' actions and to engage in more effective problem solving (Darling-Hammond & Bransford, 2005).

Metacognition is positioned at the base of the tree model as a root because without metacognition we would not be able to effectively engage in any of the DAFs. Being metacognitive involves both having metacognitive knowledge and using self-regulation, and these are both essential in order to enable us to be engaged in ongoing reflection. Metacognition enables responsiveness because facilitators who are metacognitive have a constant awareness of the situation for both themselves and others, which is paramount for effective decision-making in the work of facilitation.

How I Do It

To be metacognitive requires being constantly aware of what one is thinking, feeling, and doing and to question how reasonable these thoughts, feelings, and actions are in terms of achieving valued educational outcomes for students. In this way leaders and facilitators can continually seek to understand how they are seeing things themselves and also, importantly, how others are reacting. Reflecting on our own thinking, feelings, and actions is a part of being metacognitive. We might ask ourselves questions in the moment of facilitation, such as the following: What is happening here? How

> **"It's like having another voice in the background constantly questioning me."**
>
> (Facilitator)

am I feeling about this? What is making this difficult? How are others interpreting what is happening here? It also demands reflecting on others' reactions and asking them these questions: What is happening here for you? How are you feeling about this? What is making this difficult for you?

We can develop metacognition in others and support them to be thinking about their thinking. This may mean we are prompting and continually questioning about what is happening for others and ourselves. In this way we will have an awareness of our own thinking and decision-making that guides our actions. As well as uncovering our own reasoning, we are helping others to uncover their reasoning. This is a key action of facilitators who are metacognitive and who support others to be metacognitive.

> "It involves thinking aloud about my reasoning so both I and others are able to think about my thinking."
>
> (Facilitator)

One way of doing this is by making visible the different ways of interpreting events. Having people share their emotional response to change and their reasons for these, for example, is a start toward developing metacognition in relation to affective and emotional responses.

Facilitators who are highly metacognitive are continually checking, thinking on a number of different levels, and noticing what is going on. Effective facilitation is highly metacognitive as we seek evidence about what is happening for learners, how we as professionals might be contributing to a particular situation, and whether our efforts to change outcomes are effective.

Key Challenges for Me

Being constantly metacognitive can feel exhausting because it demands continually considering multiple perspectives. Add to this the fact that, as a facilitator, we are making decisions based on these multiple perspectives, which can be frustrating as it can slow down the pace at which we are able to work. When the going gets tough, there can be a tendency for people to want to jump to quick problem solving and make rapid decisions. Being metacognitive, however, requires constantly checking our thinking and the reactions of others to these decisions.

What I Should Notice

This is all about checking in on "being metacognitive." What are we communicating when we "think aloud," and how do we think others are interpreting this? Are we questioning ourselves as we hear our reasoning? How do we respond when others think aloud? Do we probe their thinking and encourage them to share their understanding? What do we do when people have different views? Do we notice ourselves responding more to the cognitive or to the emotional reactions of others?

Further Reading

Bransford, J., Mosborg, S., Copland, M., Honig, M., Nelson, H., Gawel, D., . . . Vye, N. (2010). Adaptive people and adaptive systems: Issues of learning and design. In A. Hargreaves, A. Lieberman, M. Fullan, & D. Hopkins (Eds.), *Second international handbook of educational change* (pp. 825–855). Dordrecht, The Netherlands: Springer.

Dumont, H., Istance, D., & Benavides, F. (Eds.). (2012). *The nature of learning: Using research to inspire practice—Practitioner guide.* Paris, France: OECD, Centre for Educational Research and Innovation. Retrieved from http://www.oecd.org/edu/ceri/50300814.pdf

Vignette 5a: Being Metacognitive

 Liam is talking with a team of teachers from fourth grade about their reading program. The teachers are focusing on the resources and planning the lessons for these new nonfiction books. Liam wants to help them think about the impact of these decisions on their learners and use that as a basis for deciding what to do.

	Louise: I think the new nonfiction books are great, and we can just put the titles into the planning template each week, which will keep that simple.
Explaining thinking and reasoning to others	*Liam:* These sound like great new resources for you. As I'm listening, I'm thinking about what effect introducing these new nonfiction books has on the students. I'm especially thinking about the students we talked about last time—the ones who are quiet in reading times, who go under the radar. I'm wondering what the impact will be for them.
	Louise: I think these books will reach everyone really.
Encouraging others to explain their thinking and reasoning	*Liam:* Tell me more about your thinking on that.
	Louise: Well, they offer a lot of choice and opportunity for independent reading. But I guess that might be more problematic for the students who aren't as good with those independent skills. *Liam:* I wonder what the students think.

Vignette 5b: Being Metacognitive

 Fran has just finished a morning meeting with department chairs at a high school. She is talking to the vice-principal about next steps. She is not sure how the session went with the department chairs as it felt as though there was some resistance to discussing assessment and feedback, and she's not sure why.

Explaining thinking and reasoning to others	*Fran:* So I'm wondering about whether we need to introduce some PL on giving feedback to learners. I wasn't sure whether I was talking about something they already knew or something they didn't want to know about today. I was thinking about how hard it is in high school environments to give feedback to individual learners about their learning and to keep focused on the students as young adults.
	Brad: I'm not sure about that. I think the department heads have a lot on their plate really, and they do a pretty good job. I don't think they'd appreciate PL on feedback.
Being aware of the consequences of actions **Encouraging others to explain their thinking and reasoning**	*Fran:* From your response I'm wondering if you saw my suggestion as a criticism. Tell me some more about what you are thinking.

(Continued)

(Continued)

	Brad: I can see what you mean, but I just think that knowing about feedback, and more holistic pedagogy things, is not really their job. They're the subject specialists. They are leading the subject. I don't think they are interested in the pedagogy so much. I'm not sure they would value that opportunity.
Explaining, thinking, and reasoning to others **Checking in about the consequences of actions**	***Fran:*** I see. I wonder what a useful next step would be then. I might be thinking in the wrong direction because I don't know this context well enough. Or maybe we need to check in with the chairs and see what they thought about today and what their ideas are about next steps. We might both be making assumptions.

Bringing a Systemic Focus

What It Is

▶ See any improvement effort as part of a number of larger contexts, which will affect how proposed changes are taken up (e.g., classroom, department, school, district, family, community).

▶ Help other people see all the "moving parts" that are involved in making improvements.

▶ Value and prioritize coherence within and across different parts of the organization.

▶ Be a coordinator and a link between levels and contexts.

▶ Explicitly develop shared understandings across levels and contexts.

▶ Focus efforts and resources on common goals.

Why It Matters

▶ Students, classrooms, and schools sit inside wider systems that shape what can be done.

▶ Isolated pockets of improvement will not lead to sustained improvement for learners, but coherence across systems can.

▶ Deliberately working across multiple levels triggers quicker and more lasting impacts.

▶ Engaging people across the system leads to better decisions and more sustainable improvement.

▶ Understanding how different layers influence what happens makes problem solving more effective.

How I Do It

▶ Build relationships with key players across the system, and gain their commitment.

▶ Keep the big picture in mind, and help others to do this too.

▶ Understand improvement in its context, seeing what surrounds the chosen focus and why things are as they are.

▶ Manage complexity, and understand how things are interconnected.

▶ Work in and across multilevel teams.

▶ Co-construct a shared vision or purpose, and keep actions across contexts and levels directed toward this.

▶ Implement specific actions as part of a wider context and broader plan.

Key Challenges for Me

▶ Preventing overload, fragmentation, and "initiativitis"

▶ Keeping the big picture in mind while also attending to details at a local level

▶ Creating coherence across systems when there are many people involved with different perceptions, commitments, and beliefs

▶ Gaining access to all levels of a context

What I Should Notice

▶ Who are the key players I need to engage with?

▶ Who is missing, and how am I including them?

▶ Where is there connection or disconnection with me?

▶ How am I making others aware of the importance of a systemic approach?

▶ How am I taking account of systemic factors in my understanding of a context or issue?

▶ Am I thinking widely when asking why things are as they are?

online resources   Available for download at https://resources.corwin.com/LeadingPowerfulPL

Bringing a Systemic Focus

What: Description of the Concept

Working systemically demands creating system-wide coherence, having an awareness of the connection (and disconnection) between parts of the system, keeping the big picture in mind, seeking to identify and understand patterns in order to manage complexity, and working in ways that have the potential to have a direct impact on multiple levels.

Effectively addressing the existing disparity of outcomes for learners demands a focus on the big picture of system-wide improvement. The experiences of students in classrooms are shaped by a series of surrounding influences: most immediately, their teacher, their peers, their families, and then their school, district, and larger community. These are subject to wider social influences too: the impacts of gender, race and poverty, and many other factors across the different contexts that surround students. Each of these influences shapes what is possible for the students, by both overt means (such as written policies, provision of resources, giving permission) and/or covert means ("how we do it here" unspoken rules, informal power hierarchies, providing personal support). The interplay among all of these people and activities means that student learning is a complex phenomenon and explains why it is not easy to make changes that affect academic and social outcomes for students (Opfer & Pedder, 2011). Bringing about system-wide improvement demands a systemic focus.

In a complex view of learning in classrooms, the different entities that are involved are termed *systems*. Schools are indeed complex systems. They comprise a number of smaller nested and interdependent systems (teacher, students, peers, teams) that are part of larger systems (districts, PL groups) and intersect with other social systems (such as health and welfare organizations, families, and community groups). Leaders and facilitators of change can increase effectiveness by bringing a systemic focus to our work and helping others to work in this way (Bryk et al., 2015).

Bringing a systemic focus demands recognizing how seemingly disparate parts of the larger system are interconnected. If serious consideration is given to the systemic nature of improvement efforts, then it becomes clear that linear thinking that is overreliant on a causal model that reduces the complexity to a series of component parts is not helpful. The concept of direct, causal, linear, and manipulable relationships among various components and systems does not work when seeking to understand the nature of learning and teaching and thus how to improve them. Instead there are dynamic and changing relationships across the systems that effect learning and teaching (Cochran-Smith, Ell, Ludlow, Grudnoff, & Aitken, 2014). For example, PL is often ineffective due to a focus on isolated issues rather than taking into account the ways in which learning is embedded in larger systems such as the professional lives of teachers and available resources in schools.

What: Description of the Root

The drive to bring a systemic focus to facilitating improvement in schools rests on two basic orientations: First, developing and prioritizing coherence around a shared purpose or vision leads to better outcomes. Second, schools really are complex entities, and interventions involving just students, just teachers, or just leaders will not lead to sustained improvement.

Bringing a systemic focus involves valuing and prioritizing coherence around a shared purpose within and across systems. We do this by promoting interactions and coordinating efforts across the organization to ensure that all stakeholders are committed to and working in accordance with a common theory for action or improvement (Fullan, 2009). By engaging students, practitioners, leaders, family and community, policy makers, and researchers in developing shared understandings as well as focusing efforts and resources on common purposes and goals, it is possible to build coherence within schools as well as across other systems that the schools may interact with (such as districts, professional development providers, or other local education providers).

Bringing a systemic focus also relies on our recognizing the complexity of schools and acknowledging that working with individuals or groups of stakeholders such as teachers will not be sufficient to create the conditions required for sustained, system-wide change. This means that we may need to work with others to develop broader teams, or to engage people who consider themselves to be "outside" the work we are doing. For example, we may need to involve senior members of school management in order to make real progress (Robinson, 2011). Using a complexity lens to understand schools also means that we have to see the link between our work and student outcomes as nonlinear and look for change in a range of ways and at different levels of the system. The quest for improved student outcomes should drive our work and shape our focus, but we need to think broadly about how improvement comes about and act at multiple levels to achieve it.

Why It Matters

Effective and long-lasting change for improvement doesn't happen by only taking into account some of the influences on students. Rather, a systemic focus is needed in which all these different influences are considered. Bringing a systemic focus involves valuing and prioritizing coherence around a shared purpose or vision, promoting interaction and coordinating efforts both within and across organizations

> "I'm now asking questions that I wouldn't have previously asked. It raises the question as to whether I had the skills needed to be productive."
>
> (Facilitator)

Leaders of change need to deliberately involve the interdependent systems that surround learners and help them develop purpose, cohesion, and ways of communicating and working together (Gilbert, 2015). Bringing a systemic focus opens up the possibility of involving family, community groups, and other support agencies such as counselors or social workers as well as the professionals embedded in the school context. A systemic focus implies that the wider the view of the system surrounding students, the better the decisions and solutions are likely to be. As leaders, this involves judicious navigation of the space between not enough voices and too many voices and the facilitation of communication between groups that may currently be "talking past each other."

Patterns of inequity, marginalization, and underachievement are systemic problems, perpetuated by local practices, expectations, and the strong influence of the status quo. Bringing a systemic focus is necessary for solving systemic problems. A systemic focus can be hard to achieve for people who are embedded in the system and can only see their piece of the puzzle. Leadership of change requires us to help widen people's understanding of the challenge they are trying to address and to work in ways that engage people at as many levels of the system as possible.

How I Do It

It is important to engage with key players across the system: it is not enough to work just with leaders, with teachers, or with families. When we begin work in a new setting a first task is to try and map out the system we are working in and understand the interdependent parts that are significant in that particular context. We can also work systemically by keeping the big picture in mind and helping others to do this too. Posing questions about how things work, or exploring why things are as they are in a broad way, can help open up new pathways for change. Reflecting back to others what we can see from our vantage point can be helpful when people are very embedded in their particular part of the school system. Once a purpose or focus is developed, leaders of change have a role in keeping action in what might seem disparate parts of the system directed toward this and working in multilevel teams to ensure that the shared vision and theory for improvement are constantly negotiated and reinforced across the various organizational levels in a school.

Bringing a systemic focus involves leaders of change zigzagging between the particular and the general: having the skill to link what is happening in a small part of the change work to the larger purpose and the eyes to see how larger influences might be shaping the particular actions taken, or not taken, at the team or classroom level.

Key Challenges for Me

One of the key challenges of bringing a systemic focus is managing the constant tension between keeping the focus on the overall purpose and taking a wide view of the challenges, while also attending to details at a local level. This can be a crucial part of our work, as people often find it very difficult to keep the big picture at front of mind when they are grappling with the realities of their day-to-day work. Explicitly modeling this balance as we work will help enable leaders and teachers to learn to do the same.

> "If we are expecting teachers to operate in a teaching as inquiry kind of mindset, addressing issues of achievement, then that needs to be modelled at all levels of the school, it needs to be modelled by me in terms of my getting better at what I do as well."
>
> (Facilitator)

Sometimes it can be challenging to gain access to all levels of a system, as some schools prefer us to work just with senior management, while some leaders devolve responsibility for PL to their deputies and don't engage at all. It can also be difficult to create coherence across the different levels within a school, particularly in large or siloed schools or in systems lacking a culture of collaboration.

Bringing a systemic focus contributes to our overall intention to keep the work manageable across all system levels and maintain a focus on a common vision so as to prevent stakeholders pursuing a string of unconnected initiatives because it seeks to tie things together and look for links. This can be challenging in busy schools where time for communication is limited.

What I Should Notice

One of the first things to notice when bringing a systemic focus to our work in schools is whether or not we have engaged the key players. This will include, but not be exclusive to, the senior management team. First of all we need to work out who they might be in this context and then find ways to engage them with the work. Developing this understanding requires sensitivity and awareness that others may work in ways that are different from what we expect. We may need to seek help from people with cultural and linguistic competencies that we do not have.

We must ask who, if anyone, is missing and how will we go about engaging and including them. This question is particularly important when we are working with students and communities with experiences differing from ours. "Nothing about us without us" is a useful catchphrase to think about in these situations. The cultural and linguistic knowledge present in students, their families, and communities could be central to improving student outcomes.

We also need to be aware of whether or not we have ensured that there is a shared vision across all system levels. The lack of a shared purpose may explain disconnection with some key players.

It is also fundamental that we notice whether or not we are making others aware of the importance of a systemic approach. Being explicit about complexity and how to manage it will equip others to do the same across all system levels.

Further Reading

Bryk, A. S., Gomez, L. M., Grunow, A., & LeMahieu, P. G. (2015). *Learning to improve: How America's schools can get better at getting better.* Cambridge, MA: Harvard Education Press.

Campbell, C., Lieberman, A., & Yashkina, A. (2018). Teacher-led professional collaboration and systemic capacity building. In A. Harris, M. Jones, & J. B. Huffman (Eds.), *Teachers leading educational reform: The power of professional learning communities* (pp. 72–85). London, England: Routledge.

Vignette 6a: Bringing a Systemic Focus

 Sofia is working with some principals from one area in her district whose schools are struggling with low student achievement assessment results in reading and writing. They have begun to offer reasons for this.

	Belinda: Well, at our school the trouble is textbooks. We just don't have enough, and the children don't respect them, so every year we need new ones and we're down to one book for two kids.
	Mark: For us it's not so much the textbooks as teachers. Our third-grade team is hopeless, and the children make no progress there, year after year. There's no PL for them.
	Lucinda: I think we'd do a lot better if we could employ more support staff. Children with special needs and non-English speakers are holding our classes back, and the teachers can't cope without support.
Seeing how things are interrelated	*Sofia:* So, I'm hearing that there are resourcing problems, of different kinds, but they are all basically about not having something you need in order to make a difference. I wonder though, since you've all got very similar patterns of achievement in your schools, what might be in common here? Can we find links between your different situations?
	Lucinda: Well, I guess we are all serving the same community, kind of—nearby communities anyway.
Keeping the big picture in mind	*Sofia:* So what do we see as the broader context for our work? How is what we are doing fitting in with our students and our social justice vision?
	Mark: I guess that matters because it looks like what we are all doing—and I don't know if it's the same or different actually—isn't really working for our children.

Vignette 6b: Bringing a Systemic Focus

F Fran is working in a large middle school. The department chairs are trying to improve student engagement in order to raise achievement. They've been doing observations in classrooms and are meeting with Fran to discuss their findings and where to go next.

	Billy: Now, in Casey's room it was a completely different story.
	Jen: It really was. Casey was amazing. The children were enraptured basically, so engaged, so focused.
	Billy: We didn't really see anything problematic, did we? After the usual "coming into the room stuff," once she started, the children were all just right there.
	Jen: I was a bit blown away really because Casey isn't really that visible in staff situations, like, you wouldn't notice her at a meeting or anything.
	Billy: It would be great to get Casey in front of other teachers actually. Maybe we could make a staff meeting dedicated to her showing some of the things she does.
	Jen: Or getting other people to go and see what we saw, having her observed and then we could have discussion groups—
	Billy: Or use the PLCs for that discussion. . . .

Keeping the big picture in mind Understanding the problem in context	**Fran:** Sounds like you had a great experience. It is wonderful to see good teachers in action. But let's take a step back. Why were we observing in classrooms? I'd like to hear about how you think Casey's work fits into the broader picture you got of the school. I think we need to understand how the pieces fit together before we think about sharing expertise.
	Billy: True, because I guess the overall message we got was that there's a lot of variation in what the children are experiencing. It's like going to different schools for some children.
Keeping actions directed toward the focus Seeing how things are interrelated	**Fran:** And that's a big picture that's worth keeping in mind as we think about the details and the actions we might take. How do we reduce that variation for our students? That might be about doing some things with Casey, but it might also be about some other actions like coteaching with some faculty members, talking to the children about how they find their teacher's approaches . . . there might be some relationship between Casey's success and the ways she's using her materials or the way she interacts with the students.
	Jen: Yeah. We need to keep connecting the dots, I guess.

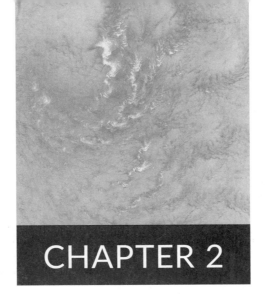

CHAPTER 2

The Trunk

Chapter 1 explored the foundational role of the roots of adaptive expertise. Moving up from the roots we come to the trunk. The trunk represents the core of adaptive expertise and why adaptive expertise matters, and it develops from the personal values and dispositions represented in roots. The three key ideas in the trunk are generative improvement, responsiveness, and relationships. See Figure 3.

Powerful professional learning (PL) that makes a difference to students and educators makes a difference because it focuses on bringing about change for improvement in a generative way that is not a one-off event but ongoing. Adaptive expertise is responsive to the needs of learners and context, so responsiveness is also central. The trunk gains its strength from the development of strong relationships through which the work is undertaken.

Even though relationships are explicit in the trunk, they are implicit in all the elements of this model of adaptive expertise. The values and dispositions in the roots influence the nature of the relationships developed through facilitation. These relationships "feed" the deliberate acts of facilitation (DAFs) that form the branches and leaves. Without the persistent and ongoing development of positive, learning-focused relationships, the DAFs will be ineffective.

Figure 3

Trunk: Responsiveness Through Relationships With a Generative Improvement Orientation

What It Is

- Notice and respond to what matters.
- Build and maintain relationships of trust, respect, and reciprocity.
- Be motivated by a relentless focus on improving valued outcomes for learners.
- Have the capacity to respond to the unknown, uncertain, and unexpected.
- Continually check if ours and others' actions lead to improvement, and respond in new ways; if not, seek to understand and to problem solve.
- Be flexible.

Why It Matters

- Responsiveness throughout an educational system drives decision-making in policy, leading, teaching, and learning for equity.
- Complex problems require educators to approach problems in flexible and novel ways.
- The quality of relationships either enables or constrains the ultimate outcomes for learners.
- Responsiveness enables educators to respond to uncertain and changing demands in their leadership, learning, and teaching.
- Intentional and focused responsiveness enables coherence and sustainability for improvement.

How I Do It

- Focus energy and resources on educational priorities.
- Maintain the focus on improvement for every learner, front and center.

- Keep all learners (including students, leaders, teachers, policy makers) in focus.
- Draw on knowledge, experience, and theories to respond differently in different contexts.
- Make opportunities for others to share their knowledge.
- Continually engage in inquiry to check if actions are responsive to the challenges faced.
- Value and respect relationships with others.

Key Challenges for Me

- Addressing tough issues that would compromise capacity for improvement
- Balancing responsiveness and flexibility in the moment with intentional planning
- Navigating task and relationship demands
- Ensuring the alignment of everyone's efforts to enable responsiveness

What I Should Notice

- How do my actions support educators to be responsive to prioritized improvement goals?
- Do my ways of responding support people to address the problem at hand?
- Which roots influence my actions, and which ones do I need to pay greater attention to?
- Am I "doing" the DAFs responsively? Which DAFs do I need to learn more about or pay greater attention to?

online resources   Available for download at https://resources.corwin.com/LeadingPowerfulPL

Responsiveness Through Relationships With a Generative Improvement Orientation

What: Description of the Trunk

> To be responsive demands being flexible and utilizing adaptive expertise.

Three key concepts are embedded in the trunk: responsiveness, relationships, and a generative improvement orientation. Like the roots they are all an essential part of adaptive expertise: they are connected, and without attention to all three, change for improvement is unlikely to be achieved or sustained.

The first concept, responsiveness, is central to the work of effective facilitators. Responsiveness is grounded in the principle that all learning must put learners at the center in ways that enable others to be responsive to their individual differences, needs, and contexts (Istance & Dumont, 2010). The ultimate goal of facilitation should always focus on improvement for students; however, as educators we have other learners to whom we must be responsive. Learners in the context of PL may also be leaders and teachers in schools, curriculum and policy developers, and district superintendents. Effective facilitation is therefore responsive to the needs of all learners, while the main focus is on students as learners; these other learners are also key.

Facilitation of learning is a social activity—how one is responsive influences and is influenced by the nature of the relationships between educators and their learners (Bryk & Schneider, 2002). Responsiveness is driven by the stances, values, and dispositions described in the roots. Quality relationships are critical, ultimately supporting or constraining the effectiveness of facilitation and the possibilities for positive outcomes for learners. Facilitators throughout the research projects emphasized the need to connect with and understand others. They talked about wanting to have genuine conversations, make connections, and get to "really know people." Quality relationships are important across all layers of the system.

Trust is paramount in relationships that support PL where relationship-based uncertainty can surface especially when new practices are tried in front of others (Nelson, Slavit, Perkins, & Hathorn, 2008). Trust allows learners to be vulnerable and feel safe when they take risks trying something new "with confidence that others will respond to their actions in positive ways, that is benevolence, reliability, competence, honesty and openness" (Forsyth, Adams, & Hoy, 2011, pp. 18–19). Trust forms through everyday actions and interactions (Bryk & Schneider, 2002) but is easily broken and difficult to repair—emphasizing the need for educators to develop and maintain trusting relationships.

Respect is also a core aspect of the trunk of adaptive expertise. Relationships of respect imply reciprocity and include the presence of trust. Genuinely respectful relationships mean that educators value the perspectives of those they work with, creating a sense of mutual safety to challenge each other as well as the knowledge of how much to challenge. Educators show respect when they recognize that others have knowledge of the particular learners and school community that they will not have.

> " . . . Ensuring that I really do try and understand what it's like for the learner whether those learners are the kids we're working with in the classroom, the teachers, or the leaders, and in terms of thinking about how do we get across to our parent community."
>
> (Facilitator)

The development of reciprocal relationships is essential to working effectively not only with leaders and teachers in PL situations but also with learners and their families—especially those from different cultural worldviews and languages. Reciprocal relationships require those with power to create opportunities for the reciprocal sharing of knowledge that builds from a strengths-based approach that is deliberately using the expertise in the room.

Although we can't do this work alone and relationships are key, relationships are not enough for educational improvement, which is why the trunk also represents a generative improvement orientation. Relationships need to be focused on improvement for learners and generate focus and energy toward seeking equity in outcomes for our most vulnerable learners. Collaborative professionalism is central to the types of relationship that are represented in the trunk. Collaborative professionalism (Hargreaves & Shirley, 2018) is composed of "forms of collaboration among educators that are professional in the sense of being open, rigorous, challenging and evidence-informed" (p. 82).

At the heart of a generative improvement orientation is the notion that improvement is an ongoing endeavor in which we get closer and closer to valued and desired educational outcomes and goals. One of the challenges of educational improvement, however, is that change is inherent and nothing is stagnant, including desired outcomes and goals, so striving for improvement within a generative improvement orientation might be considered an organic process as we continually reflect on, evaluate, and fine-tune approaches to our work.

Responsiveness with a generative improvement orientation is enabled by relationships of trust, respect, and reciprocity yet at the same time made more complex by the need to drive improvement alongside developing and maintaining relationships. Relationships are important because facilitation is about changing practice and holding a generative improvement orientation. This requires a relentless focus on improving valued outcomes for all student-learners—especially those who are currently underserved by our education systems.

Educators are tasked with responding to unknown, uncertain, and often unexpected situations with multiple goals being worked toward simultaneously. Responsiveness demands responding in new ways to avoid the pitfalls of past improvement efforts that have not led to generative, sustained, and systemic improvement (Cuban, 2015). This requires educators to continuously notice and seek to understand what matters and take action to solve problems. Responsiveness demands they are able to acquire and use deep conceptual understanding to create new solutions to existing problems and innovative solutions to new problems (Hatano & Inagaki, 1986).

Why It Matters

Responsiveness needs to be evident at all levels of an organization for systemic and sustainable improvement (Elmore, 2004). Considering the complexity of a classroom and then scaling that up to the complexity of systems, one can see how important responsiveness is and the complex roles facilitators have. Facilitators of PL have key roles in enabling responsiveness through not only their work with leaders, teachers, and students but also in the policy arena as their work affects the larger design and planning for effective facilitation.

Empowering relationships form a strong base for successful learning. "Emerging and strengthening evidence indicates that leadership is relational, and is an influence process on successful learning relationships that are reciprocal, collaborative and empowering for all parties [to] have an impact on student engagement, achievement and well-being" (Timperley & Robertson, 2011, p. 8). However, empowering relationships by themselves are unlikely to lead to change for improvement.

> *"Effective facilitation needs to result in the improvement of not only single classrooms or schools, but also school systems."*
>
> (Elmore, 2004)

Effective facilitators of PL recognize the importance of relationships and that the context of learning has an impact on teachers' willingness to take risks and change their practice (Twyford, 2016). In Twyford's 2016 study, facilitators reported deliberately building relationships to facilitate change. In this same study, teachers also recognized the importance of relationships. For them, trust, security, and confidentiality in their relationships with leaders and facilitators were linked to decreasing perceived risk and increased the likelihood of them trying new practices. These relationships included "notions of being known as a learner, being shown empathy and respect, feeling supported, and feeling trust" (Twyford, 2016, p. 109).

A generative improvement orientation means being responsive in ways that continually drive improvement. Generative improvement involves facilitating for improvement that goes beyond creating isolated pockets of success and promotes ongoing improvement within and across systems (Chrispeels & Gonzalez, 2006). Generative improvement is ongoing and goal focused.

Leaders and facilitators have a key role in supporting educators to respond to uncertain and changing demands in their leadership, learning, and teaching. Intentional and focused responsiveness enables coherence and sustainability in improvement efforts on a system-wide level. Responsiveness through relationships with a generative improvement orientation is needed throughout an educational system to drive decision-making in policy, leading, teaching, and learning (Elmore, 2004).

How I Do It

> "If you want to be a really, really good facilitator, which is using adaptive expertise, you have to do all of those [roots and DAFs], but you do them in special combinations and put them out at the right moment and contextually administer a lot of other things."
>
> (Facilitator)

The trunk represents a collaborative process. We are responsive through relationships with a generative improvement orientation when we build relationships while simultaneously being responsive to the needs of all learners including leaders, teachers, and students as well as when we focus our own and others' efforts and resources on educational priorities. Identifying key priorities is important, and keeping the focus on improvement for students front and center matters.

Being responsive demands drawing on knowledge, experience, and theories as we respond differently in different contexts. Drawing on our knowledge, theories, and experiences in ways that allow us to respond in uncertain and complex situations is key to effective facilitation.

Inquiry is a key part of the work of facilitators. Questions to consider include the following: How am I enacting the DAFs in my work with this school? What DAFs are or are not my strengths? What might I need to focus on more to make a bigger difference in this school? How do I know if I am making a difference? How am I building and maintaining relationships— are they trusting, respectful, and reciprocal? Continually engaging in inquiry is critical to check if educators' actions are responsive to the challenges faced by the learners with whom they are working.

Key Challenges for Me

To be responsive, one has to be able to be flexible, to problem solve, and to reflect in action (Schön, 1983). It also demands being both able and willing to respond to the unexpected and sometimes being uncomfortable. One of the key challenges of responsiveness is the risk of compromising the capacity for improvement due to a reluctance or fear of tackling tough issues because of the potential effect on relationships or not responding to the unexpected or uncomfortable. It can be a challenge to deliberately make visible and discuss difficult issues and engage in genuine inquiry rather than ignore or avoid the tough issues. It is essential to be aware of the possible pitfalls; being responsive is more than making people feel better, which can result in masking or shifting the problem. However, such a response would not be viewed as being within a generative improvement orientation.

Ensuring the alignment of efforts to enable responsiveness can be a challenge in a policy climate with a tendency for overload. Facilitators of learning have an important role in focusing energy and resources on educational priorities and noticing and avoiding distractions.

What I Should Notice

There are many ways to be responsive. What matters is that we as educators are continually checking that we are responsive and that we are supporting the educators we work with to be responsive to the needs of their learners and the prioritized concerns that are the focus of the work. We might ask if our ways of responding address the prioritized problem at hand and help leaders and teachers to continually inquire into the effectiveness of their own actions by asking this same question. We can also check that all and not some of the "roots" influence our work. Which roots are we overreliant on, and which ones do we need to pay greater attention to and learn more about. For example, are we being metacognitive when responding to the emotion in the context and considering our impact on others? Are we being responsive when we decide which DAFs to focus on, or do we focus on the ones we feel we have greatest expertise in?

Effective facilitators are aware both of their own capacity to be responsive and also of their capacity to support others to be responsive. To be responsive requires continually checking progress toward valued outcomes and so too is the extent to which we attend to the complex, multiple, and systemic layers of action needed for generative improvement.

Further Reading

Bryk, A. S., Gomez, L. M., Grunow, A., & LeMahieu, P. G. (2015). *Learning to improve: How America's schools can get better at getting better.* Cambridge, MA: Harvard Education Press.

Hargreaves, A., & Shirley, D. (2018). *Leading from the middle: Spreading learning, well-being and identity across Ontario: Council of Ontario Directors of Education report.* Ontario, Canada: Council of Ontario Directors of Education. Retrieved from http://ccsli.ca/downloads/2018-Leading_From_the_Middle_Final-EN.pdf

Vignette a: Responsiveness Through Relationships With a Generative Improvement Orientation

 Fran is talking to colleagues over lunch. One colleague is new to facilitation work in schools and is worried that in one school she has developed relationships that are too friendly. She seems to have become more of a listening ear than an agent of change. Fran advises her.

Fran: There's a fine line that you have to walk between getting to know people, really building a relationship with them, and keeping the students at the core and asking the difficult questions at times. It's easy to turn up and have a chat and update each other with where people are—and sometimes they're really upset or distressed and you have to deal with that—but as the leader you have to also keep coming back to what's at the center: the students and their learning. So you have to respond to what's going on, maintain and build relationships . . . and be focused on improvement. Sometimes it's hard to know which way to jump.

Vignette b: Responsiveness Through Relationships With a Generative Improvement Orientation

 Liam is talking to a principal about shifting his work away from one-off workshops toward working with schools on inquiry into their learners' literacy experiences and how these can be improved.

Liam: I find that our new way of working—alongside teachers on inquiry—is allowing me to build relationships with teams and get to understand their context more than I could in a workshop situation. This way I can pick up on what matters in that particular school and maybe divert from my "plan" in order to pick up on something significant. It's not that I don't prepare; it's more that I'm prepared for several different things and am prepared to follow something that comes up rather than shut it down because it wasn't "on the list."

Vignette c: Responsiveness Through Relationships With a Generative Improvement Orientation

 Penny is talking at a new principals' group meeting at her district, explaining how she is trying to balance the need to develop relationships with the need to speak out about what needs to change and why—and what she might need to learn in order to do this.

Penny: I've been working on building relationships in this new school. You don't just get given respect, especially when you come from outside an area, so I'm trying to build trust and mutual respect. I'm aware, though, that at times I'm backing off something that I think is really important in order to maintain a relationship, and I think I need to learn more about how to address those things while keeping the relationship going. Being a principal requires some bravery, but for me it's the children who must always come first, and I think I have that in common with the teachers, deep down.

Vignette d: Responsiveness Through Relationships With a Generative Improvement Orientation

 Mateo is talking to his principal about how he is developing his role as department chair. For him, a key part of being responsive is to learn together with his team while trying to communicate a generative improvement orientation.

Mateo: I was one of the team before, but now that I'm the department chair it's a bit different. Relationships change when you are the boss. I miss being part of the team, but now I can see a whole lot more about our work and how it fits into the school and how it fits in with the students' lives that I didn't see when I was just teaching whoever came through the door. I somehow have to convey that to my team, making it clear that we have a moral duty with these students and that they must be at the heart of what we do without the teachers saying "He's gotten too big for his boots now that he's chair." So, I'm trying to work alongside, put my own practice on the line, seek help—show that I'm vulnerable and that we're learning together—and I'm trying not to jump too far ahead in my own mind. I keep coming back to who I'm working with and what they need and respond to that.

Vignette e: Responsiveness Through Relationships With a Generative Improvement Orientation

S Sofia is explaining the new PL model that her district has adopted to other superintendents from her city. She is emphasizing how relationships and responsiveness are critical at all levels of an organization—and that a generative improvement orientation is central to improving outcomes for learners.

Sofia: When you have a district-level overview, it's easy to just look at numbers and forget that they represent people. I don't have the time to meet everyone or know them personally, so it's tempting just to deal with issues as though they were problems that didn't involve people's lives—more cut and dried than getting involved. But I think at all levels of an organization you have to model what you want, what you expect. So in my sphere of influence (with my immediate team) I want to build relationships and trust, and beyond that I want trust and reciprocity so I can get good feedback on my performance and so I get told when things go wrong! I'm responsible for the direction of our district, so there's lots of high-level strategy stuff involved, but we can't get so locked in that we can't respond to things that happen. We need structures that are responsive; like our new PL model, the model is set in place, but it's an inherently responsive model, so it provides flexibility as part of how it works. And, of course, the whole thing has improvement for children at the center. That's what we're here for after all.

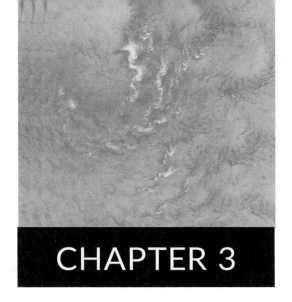

CHAPTER 3

Branches and Leaves

This chapter describes deliberate acts of facilitation (DAFs) that are used by effective facilitators. In the tree metaphor, these DAFs are the leaves. Leaves are produced by healthy trees with strong roots and trunks. They rely on roots and trunks for sustenance and support. Twelve DAFs are presented in this chapter. These DAFs emerged from the research with effective facilitators (please see the Research Appendix for more information about how they were developed). You may have others—relevant to your context—that you could add to this model as you work with educators in your setting.

The DAFs are organized into three branches, or clusters, of the tree: purpose and focus, knowledge and inquiry, and effective learning processes. These branches help to organize the DAFs and make them easier to access. In this chapter each branch is briefly introduced then followed by the appropriate DAFs. We have used the same format as we used for the roots and trunk; each DAF has a summary, extended explanation, Further Reading section, and brief example vignettes. The twelve DAFs, and the branches, are listed here:

Purpose and Focus

1. Clarifying purpose

2. Focusing on valued student outcomes

3. Building coherence

4. Creating commitment and taking action

Knowledge and Inquiry

5. Deepening knowledge

6. Using evidence critically

7. Using focused and deep collaborative inquiry

Effective Learning Processes

    8. Surfacing and engaging theories and beliefs

    9. Navigating perceptions of risk

   10. Developing self-regulation

   11. Providing appropriate support and challenge

   12. Co-constructing learning

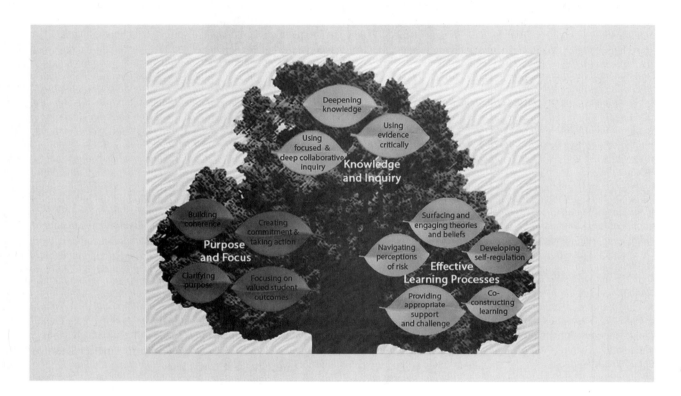

Branch 1. Purpose and Focus

The first cluster of DAFs center on purpose and focus. Schools and other education settings are usually very busy places. They are also fundamentally complex, which makes them hard to understand. As a consequence, it is easy for a lot of energy to be dissipated across multiple projects—and day-to-day crises provide further distraction. The four DAFs on this "branch" describe DAFs that help leaders and others settle on a purpose and "keep the main thing the main thing." They are explained separately to show their importance. They provide leaders of learning with sufficient detail to enact; however, they may need to be worked on simultaneously and not considered as discrete acts to tackle in a linear order.

The four DAFs centered on purpose and focus are as follows:

1. Clarifying purpose
2. Focusing on valued student outcomes
3. Building coherence
4. Creating commitment and taking action

Clarifying Purpose

What It Is

▶ Clarify the overarching purpose of improving all learner outcomes to create a focus toward which everyone works on a day-to-day basis.

▶ Develop a deep understanding of the overarching purpose from which to focus specific actions.

▶ Link actions to the central purpose of the work.

▶ Co-construct the process of clarifying purpose.

▶ Ensure a relentless focus on learners by being "keepers of the purpose."

Why It Matters

▶ An explicit shared clear purpose provides direction and avoids dissipating the limited time and energy available in schools.

▶ An overarching purpose, driven by a social justice motivation, keeps the work going when things get tough.

▶ A narrow and deep approach that is explicitly designed for transfer to other areas is more effective than doing many things at once.

▶ Schools are busy places, and educators can need encouragement and permission to focus on a few key things.

How I Do It

▶ Work closely with leaders and teachers to co-construct and clarify a shared purpose.

▶ Be keepers of the purpose. Point out drift from the focus to those who may be too close to the work to see it. Name the purpose to remind leaders at key times.

▶ Relate and deliberately link all actions back to the purpose and current focus.

▶ Check in with others about purpose and ask these questions: How does this fit with what we are doing? Why are we doing this? What will be the impact on learners?

Key Challenges for Me

▶ Making sure that purpose is co-constructed in genuine ways by those tasked with making the changes

▶ Getting a shared and deep understanding of equity necessary for improving all learner outcomes through changing educator practices

▶ Remembering to regularly and explicitly return to the purpose

▶ Staying strong as the keeper of the purpose even when there is disagreement

What I Should Notice

▶ How clearly can people articulate the purpose and the reasons for the activities being undertaken?

▶ Is the school or district channeling its energy and time into work that is part of the agreed purpose, or are there many distractions?

▶ Is the main focus becoming part of "how we do things" rather than an add-on or optional extra?

▶ Is there a relentless focus on improving learner outcomes?

  Available for download at https://resources.corwin.com/LeadingPowerfulPL

Clarifying Purpose

What: Description of the Concept

The overarching purpose of taking an adaptive expertise approach to the facilitation of improvement in schools is to improve outcomes for all learners—in particular those who are not well served by their education systems. This means the purpose must be responsive to the context and the learner's culture and intended to achieve transformative change, not tweaking the status quo. The purpose is driven by valued student outcomes that, in this framework, are broadly conceived to include academic, social and emotional well-being, engagement and participatory outcomes, and also outcomes valued by families and communities. Social justice and improving equity are the fundamental purposes of school improvement. Keeping this purpose clear, shared, and understood by everyone is a key element of facilitation.

> *It is important to reframe the presenting problem in terms of the purpose of the PL, particularly keeping the focus on the students and their learning.*

What: Description of the Deliberate Act of Facilitation

Clarifying purpose with those tasked to make the changes means unpacking the "main thing" where the main thing is improving student outcomes.

The overarching purpose drives where to plan the focus of educator actions. Clarifying the specific focus of the work together is a strategic action of facilitation, as the plan of work becomes clear and shared, increasing the likelihood of successful change and importantly, prevents everyone from becoming overwhelmed by the size and scope of the task. Attempting to address outcomes in too many learning areas simultaneously is unlikely to be effective. Once success has been achieved in one aspect of students' learning, the focus can become the transfer of effective practices to other areas of learning.

It is essential to have an overarching purpose and agreed-upon specific focus to deliberately return to as leaders and teachers may become distracted by daily or urgent demands, can't see why change is necessary, or start to focus on other issues and forget the central thrust of the work we are doing. This can involve clarifying misconceptions and confusions that have arisen or going deeper into the work as needed along the way. Sometimes leaders and teachers need facilitators to be keepers of the purpose, acting as a conscience for them regarding student learning. This can be a support for them, particularly when other people and organizations may be vying for school attention and resources, which distracts from the main purpose. A relentless focus on learners, accompanied by a deep understanding of and commitment to social justice, is needed to embed real change in schools.

> "It's about student learning and, as leaders, if there are potential issues or problems . . . how are you going to work out strategies to ensure that whatever we do has an impact on student learning? That's the key thing."
>
> (Facilitator)

Why It Matters

A clear sense of purpose, linked to specific foci and actions, keeps the focus on learners, sustains motivation, and avoids energy becoming dissipated (Timperley, Kaser, & Halbert, 2014). Research on teaching for transfer suggests that a narrow and deep approach that is explicitly designed for transfer to other areas is more effective than doing many things at once (Bryk, Sebring, Kerbow, Rollow, & Easton, 1998). Trying to do too much at once requires excessive amounts of unsustainable energy and often creates burnout, typically with little demonstrable effect. It is not uncommon to find schools focusing on achieving wide-ranging impact rather than using a narrow focus.

If the overarching purpose is not focused on improving student learning for all students, then change work might serve to exacerbate differences between the students who are doing well and those who are not, rather than ameliorate them (Cochran-Smith & Lytle, 2009). Proposed actions, hunches, and ideas need to be tested against the purpose of improving outcomes for marginalized learners to ensure that change improves valued educational outcomes for everyone.

How I Do It

Spending time co-constructing understanding of the overarching purpose is necessary to getting long-term commitment and shared vision. Working out how the purpose looks in each school context makes it real for the leaders and teachers. Facilitators can help keep the purpose front and center by reminding leaders and teachers of their shared purpose, especially when decisions seem to be drifting away from the focus. Asking questions such as "How does this link to our purpose?" and "How will this help us improve outcomes for our marginalized learners?" at key points could be effective. These questions reinforce why the changes are important. Being explicit about how all actions link to the shared purpose keeps work on track.

> *Co-constructing meaning in particular situations helps to clarify purpose and improve communication.*

Key Challenges for Me

There are two points in time at which clarifying purpose poses particular challenges: at the beginning of working with a new school and once work has been under way for some time. At the beginning of new work with a school, it can be challenging to get a shared understanding and commitment to the overarching purpose and how the proposed actions might address that purpose. Leaders and staff may not see the urgency or necessity for change, or they may not believe that working with a facilitator using knowledge and inquiry-building methods will make a substantive difference for learners. This can be particularly uncomfortable when discussing social justice and equitable outcomes as these discussions may surface deep-seated biases and deficit thinking. Making sure that a school-based interpretation of the purpose is genuinely co-constructed can be a key challenge in these circumstances.

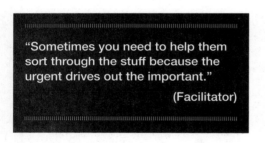

"Sometimes you need to help them sort through the stuff because the urgent drives out the important."

(Facilitator)

As work proceeds, it is important to remember to come back to the purpose frequently. It is easy to get busy and distracted and to forget to check and make sure that actions are still aligned with the overarching goal. Keeping the purpose front and center in everyone's minds helps to embed the new ways of working.

What I Should Notice

If the overarching purpose is agreed, then leaders and teachers will be able to articulate the purpose and the reasons for various activities being undertaken. This may need prompting at the start; however, over time leaders and teachers will start to work as though the purpose is embedded in their thinking and an accepted part of how the school works rather than an aim imposed from outside the school or by leaders within the school. Remember to check whether leaders and teachers see themselves as advocates of social justice. If this is not present, then concepts of equity will need to be surfaced and engaged as improvement outcomes will be compromised.

Facilitators should notice that activity in the school should become increasingly focused and explicitly aligned with the overarching purpose. When purpose is clear, a sense of urgency about improving learner outcomes will become the focus of professional discussion and professional learning (PL) as well as classroom practice.

Further Reading

Robinson, V. M. J. (2011). *Student-centered leadership*. San Francisco, CA: Jossey-Bass.

Timperley, H., Kaser, L., & Halbert, J. (2014). *A framework for transforming learning in schools: Innovation and the spiral of inquiry*. Melbourne, Australia: Centre for Strategic Education.

Vignette 1a: Clarifying Purpose

 Penny is working with her teachers in a staff meeting. They are talking about the teaching and learning of reading because their inquiry focus is accelerating students' progress in reading. Penny is aware that while the teachers might know that the focus is on reading, they are probably not clear on what the overall goal might be, so there is a risk that their efforts will be piecemeal and not address the issues evident in the student data.

Co-constructing clarification of purpose	**Penny:** So, let's see if we can express our central concern, our main thing, as a question that could help us focus our inquiry. What do you think is the overall goal?
	Maria: I guess it's to get better results in reading, raise achievement, you know, higher scores . . .
	David: I think it's about changing our practice, being more engaging—better reading materials, more relevance.
Co-constructing clarification of purpose Keeping the focus on learners	**Penny:** So, there's two pieces there: student achievement and teaching practice. I think one of the issues that feeds into both of those ideas is low rate of progress. Have a look at the data. Their results are trending lower over the past three years. Is it the kids or maybe the approaches we are taking?
	Diana: That's true. It's harder to see that when you are looking at a list of scores. It doesn't really show their overall progess. I guess it's important to look at different sources of data. Could our overall goal be to address that trend somehow? Make progress quicker?
	David: Accelerate progress.
	Diana: Yeah, accelerate—we could try a few things to do that.
Co-constructing clarification of purpose	**Penny:** So, you are saying that our overall goal could be to accelerate progress in reading, and then we could work on different strategies that might contribute to that goal? A question might be this: What teaching techniques accelerate progress in reading?
	Maria: It might be broader if we say "How can we accelerate progress in reading?" because it might not just be teaching techniques. It might be sharing with parents or something.
Co-constructing clarification of purpose Keeping the focus on learners	**Penny:** Sure. So, our overall purpose is to accelerate progress in reading. Great! That comes from the data and focuses on our learners. We could make a big difference doing this together.

Vignette 1b: Clarifying Purpose

Fran is visiting a middle school that she hasn't been into for a semester. She is checking in with the principal (Mark) and leadership team to see how they are going with implementing inquiry as part of their staff PL strategy. Their meeting begins with a presentation by the department chair for science (Pamela) about the introduction of new robotics materials and software into the sixth-grade science classes. Fran becomes aware that the team has moved away from the central purpose it had agreed on last time she visited.

	Pamela: All in all, I'm really pleased with the response from the teachers, and the students love it, of course—new and different, and very hands on.
	Mark: It looks fantastic, what a great initiative. I wouldn't mind getting to play with it myself. I'm really glad we invested in this—and proud of the staff for the way they have taken it on.
Keeping the focus on the overall purpose **Trying to link actions to the central purpose**	**Fran:** It looks amazing, and clearly everyone has really enjoyed doing it. How does this fit in with what we've been looking at? With the use of inquiry? Was it part of that work?
	Mark: Well, not really. It kind of came up as an opportunity to purchase the equipment, and so we went ahead with it.
	Pamela: It certainly relates to the students doing inquiry. It's all focused around problem solving and trying things out.
Keeping the focus on the overall purpose **Focusing on learners** **Developing deep understanding of the purpose**	**Fran:** Okay, so let's look back at what we were talking about last time we were together, about PL. Tell me about what you've done in that area. Our overall purpose was to implement teacher inquiry in order to raise student achievement, focusing on science. Maybe we need to look again at the difference between teaching through inquiry and inquiry into teaching—it can be hard to get a hold of to start with.

Focusing on Valued Student Outcomes

DAF #2

What It Is

▶ Ensure a consistent focus on outcomes for all students.

▶ Consider student learning and well-being holistically, and define valued student outcomes accordingly.

▶ Ensure there is a shared understanding of the nature of valued outcomes for all learners.

▶ Focus specifically on success for all learners, especially those currently underserved.

▶ Make a difference for all learners by constantly checking for improvements.

Why It Matters

▶ Improving outcomes for each and every learner is the primary purpose of PL.

▶ A shared understanding of valued outcomes provides direction.

▶ A focus on valued student outcomes drives responsiveness, motivation, and a shared purpose.

▶ A focus on valued student outcomes involves co-constructing what that means for every learner.

▶ A shared definition of valued student outcomes is the benchmark against which the impact of PL is measured.

How I Do It

▶ Seek clarity on what valued outcomes are for all learners.

▶ Confirm valued outcomes are shared and understood by all.

▶ Ensure an unrelenting focus on improving outcomes for students.

▶ Connect all decisions and actions to implications for learners, particularly diverse learners' needs.

▶ Ensure that leaders and teachers learn how to keep student outcomes central to all decisions and actions.

▶ Apply an evaluative lens to measuring impact of PL on valued student outcomes.

Key Challenges for Me

▶ Getting people on the same page regarding what specific valued student outcomes are

▶ Keeping the main thing the main thing

▶ Defining valued outcomes holistically

▶ Defining the area of focus based on evidence and inquiry into student competencies and needs

What I Should Notice

▶ Is there consensus on the nature of valued outcomes, particularly for linguistically diverse learners?

▶ Do leaders and teachers link all actions and decisions back to valued student outcomes?

▶ Is the impact of changed practice on valued student outcomes being measured?

Available for download at https://resources.corwin.com/LeadingPowerfulPL

Focusing on Valued Student Outcomes

What: Description of the Concept

Improving student outcomes—particularly for learners from different cultures, languages, and socioeconomic circumstances—is the core business of PL. Valued outcomes go beyond the academic outcomes traditionally measured to include nonacademic outcomes such as well-being, learner competencies, and social-emotional skills. A specific shared focus on success for each learner is essential to improving educational experiences and outcomes for all learners.

What: Description of the Deliberate Act of Facilitation

Right from the start, it is important that we define and agree on what valued student outcomes will be in the context of the PL, as we cannot assume we will all agree. What we as individuals value is informed by who we are, such as our culture, gender, and prior experiences. Broad shifts in what is valued can also occur over time, as seen in the worldwide shift away from a single focus on standardized test results.

> *"In a democracy, desired outcomes from an education system are and should be subject to a contested and evolving discourse about what parents and wider communities want for all our learners."*
>
> (Timperley & Alton-Lee, 2008, p. 336)

While academic achievement is crucial for success in life, student learning and well-being must be considered holistically, and it is important to take this into account when defining valued student outcomes. It is also imperative to consider and co-construct what success looks like for linguistically and culturally diverse learners and to ensure that there is a shared understanding of the nature of these valued outcomes for all learners across the school.

Constantly checking for improvement by measuring the impact of changed practices will ensure that only those actions that will have an impact on valued student outcomes are prioritized because linking all decisions and actions back to their implications for diverse learners' needs and progress will ensure that the focus and the activity undertaken in a school are centered on improving outcomes for learners.

Why It Matters

Valued outcomes include several factors: expectations from curriculum, student learning and well-being needs, and family and community values. Academic learning is the core business of schooling and ensuring that all students perform and progress through the curriculum areas of reading, writing, and mathematics will keep them on track to achieve success at school and in later life. However, this is not happening for all learners, particularly for learners from different cultures, languages, and socioeconomic circumstances.

> *"Learners [work] with others to determine successful educational pathways, realizing their cultural distinctiveness and potential."*
>
> (Robinson, Hohepa, & Lloyd, 2009, p. 73)

But valued student outcomes need not, and should not, be defined solely in terms of academic performance. Worldwide we have visions for children and young people that see them grow into confident, connected, actively involved, and lifelong learners. While academic achievement in literacy and numeracy is central to this vision, it is not the only defining factor for success. Valuing and respecting the cultural identity of indigenous learners is also crucial as learners hold multiple identities. To be successful, indigenous learners cannot be asked to turn their backs on their own cultures. They must be citizens of their own cultures, their countries, and the world.

In many jurisdictions across the world, educators are asking how achievement can be considered alongside learners' well-being and identity (Hargreaves & Shirley, 2018). It is important for any school or district, and any

PL work, to consider and co-construct with teachers, students, and families what constitutes valued outcomes for all learners in their context.

A focus on what valued student outcomes look like for culturally and linguistically diverse learners drives a responsive approach to PL. It is important that we consider how to enable all students to achieve success in culturally sustaining ways and to ensure that all stakeholders share and participate in that vision: one that is holistic and considers student learning, identity, language, culture, and well-being, knowing the learner and the strengths they bring to the learning context. Shared understanding of valued outcomes will provide direction for the improvement effort in schools and drive responsiveness and motivation as well as provide a strong sense of shared purpose.

A shared, co-constructed definition of valued student outcomes for all learners will inform the focus for inquiry and the plan of action for the PL and provide a benchmark against which all actions will be measured. All activities within the PL should begin with a clear vision of valued student outcomes, and all actions taken should be measured in terms of their impact on these outcomes.

How I Do It

We can ensure an unrelenting focus on improving outcomes for students by linking all decisions and actions back to their implications for the needs of students, particularly priority learners. We can also ensure a holistic and culturally responsive definition of valued student outcomes by seeking clarity from leaders, teachers, learners, and families on how success is defined for linguistically and culturally diverse students. This will ensure we don't make assumptions about how others think about valued student outcomes.

We can also ensure a sustainable approach to focusing on valued student outcomes by explicitly linking decisions and actions back to student outcomes. Keeping the connection between the activities undertaken in schools and the valued outcomes that are the objective of learning front of mind for leaders and teachers will enable them to continue to make this connection outside of the context of the PL. It is also important that we enable leaders and teachers to apply an evaluative lens to measuring the impact of PL on valued student outcomes.

> "You can respect and love [students] to bits and all the rest of it, but it's actually about shifting that so that you are involved in the learning and understanding what they value, their families' value, so they do achieve what they want to achieve."
>
> (Facilitator)

Key Challenges for Me

It can be a challenge to maintain everyone's focus and keep the main thing the main thing in a busy school environment where distractions abound. All too often, PL can be relegated to the status of an optional extra. When we consciously and explicitly link all decisions and actions back to their impact on valued student outcomes, it reminds all stakeholders of the end in mind and of the importance of the work.

Defining valued student outcomes holistically for all learners, and achieving consensus on those definitions, can be challenging because there are a number of stakeholders to consult. In addition, schools are linguistically and culturally diverse, so there will be a number of ways of understanding and defining valued outcomes.

> "So, they think that they do everything exceptionally well, but it's still about them as teachers. They have not really factored that it's about the students. So, when I start saying it's about students, not them, well that is when it gets challenging."
>
> (Facilitator)

It may also be challenging to delineate a narrow and deep area of focus once the nature of valued student outcomes has been agreed on. The focus should be based on a careful diagnosis of student competencies and needs within the context of agreed valued outcomes. This is necessary to avoid basing actions on educators' assumptions of the problem, which commonly limit change.

What I Should Notice

It is important to notice whether there is consensus among all stakeholders as to the definition of valued student outcomes, particularly for linguistically and culturally diverse learners, and that those outcomes include both academic and more holistic measures. How do leaders and teachers understand and talk about equity and social justice? How do leaders and teachers integrate their academic and well-being goals?

It is also important to notice whether or not leaders and teachers keep the main thing the main thing. Are all actions and decisions deliberately linked back to valued student outcomes or whether the focus has become diluted and superficial? Finally, it is crucial to notice if the impact of changed practices is being measured against the agreed valued outcomes and to take note of whether or not teachers and leaders have the evaluative capacity to accurately make those judgments. If not, then it will be necessary to build this capability.

Further Reading

Si'ilata, R. K., Wendt Samu, T., & Siteine, A. (2017). The Va'atele framework: Redefining and transforming Pasifika education. In E. McKinley & L. Tuhiwai Smith (Eds.), *The handbook of indigenous education*. Singapore: Springer. doi:10.1007/978-981-10-1839-8_34-1

Timperley, H., Kaser, L., & Halbert, J. (2014). *A framework for transforming learning in schools: Innovation and the spiral of inquiry.* Melbourne, Australia: Centre for Strategic Education.

Vignette 2a: Focusing on Valued Student Outcomes

S Sofia is working with a group of elementary school principals from her district, looking at the district's PL offerings and how they can move from external providers to using inquiry. She is aware that some principals have tried using an inquiry approach with their staff, so she has invited them in to talk about what they've done and how it is going—and to plan how they might move forward as a district.

	Sofia: So, we are trying to move our PL to learning through inquiry, collaborating within our schools and across the district. What do you think we need to do first? We've already got some things happening in your schools. That's why you're here!
	Alyssa: I think we need to look at teachers' mathematical knowledge for teaching. We started using an inquiry approach, but the teachers just didn't know enough.
	Martin: We had a similar experience. We started looking at how we teach writing, but there weren't enough people who knew what or how to change. It just faded out.
Focusing consistently on outcomes for learners	***Sofia:*** Interesting. So, tell us about the student learning challenges you were facing? How did you decide on these areas?
	Alyssa: Well, we hadn't looked at math for a few years, so we thought it was time for some more input or focus.
Focusing consistently on outcomes for learners	***Sofia:*** How about the students? What did you know about students and mathematics?
	Alyssa: I guess we didn't really think about that much. I mean, our math results haven't changed much over the years.
	Martin: I don't find the results easy to use actually, not in the form we get them in.

Having a holistic view of outcomes	**Sofia:** Although there are other sources of evidence, not just the standardized test results.
	Martin: That's true, but I'm not sure where they would be.
Focusing consistently on outcomes for learners	**Sofia:** I wonder if maybe the first thing we need to do, in PL, is learn something about evidence of student outcomes and what we can learn from that. For interpreting types of evidence, we need to make sure that whatever we do is focused on an understanding of the impact on students.
	Alyssa: That would be a change for us, but it might work.
	Martin: It gets that link through to the students going right from the start, I guess.

Vignette 2b: Focusing on Valued Student Outcomes

 Mateo is meeting with his math department to talk about their upcoming work on geometry with the Grade 7 students. The curriculum for geometry is extensive, and the math department always struggles for time and rarely gets through everything. Mateo wants to make choices as a team about what are the most valuable outcomes for their students.

	Mateo: So, geometry. What do we want to do here?
	Thomas: I'm keen to try some of the new software programs with the seventh graders. I think they will make teaching some of the angle work much easier as the students can manipulate the lines more easily than drawing with a pencil and paper.
	Elisa: There's that great task on vertical angles in the textbook too—the one we did last year that really got them interested.
Focusing consistently on outcomes for learners	**Mateo:** Sounds like we've got some good ideas already. How about we start by looking at what we want the students to know and be able to do? Then we can match up our resource ideas to the key concepts.
	Thomas: Well, that's basically outlined in the Common Core really.
Focusing consistently on outcomes for learners **Establishing what valued outcomes are for these learners**	**Mateo:** Yeah, but I think it would help us to work out what this group of students really need so we can tackle the key ideas, not just go for covering the curriculum. What are the outcomes that we think are really important for this group?
	Maria: Well, actually, part of it is confidence. Confidence to apply what they know to new problems. They might be able to do all the angle examples, but then we see a surface area problem in context they're too scared to try.
Having a holistic view of what valued outcomes are **Building a shared understanding of the nature of valued outcomes**	**Mateo:** So, one of the outcomes we are looking for is confidence . . . What might that look like? I wonder, if they had more confidence, what might we see?

DAF #3

Building Coherence

What It Is

▶ Develop alignment between activity across all levels of the system, from classrooms to principal's office and ideally to the district office.

▶ Work to align documents, actions, evidence gathering, analysis, and conceptual frameworks to build a coherent picture.

▶ Develop a principled rather than ad hoc approach.

▶ Use theories and frameworks as appropriate.

Why It Matters

▶ When there is visible coherence, with all educators and their community seeing where things fit together, confusion and inertia will be reduced.

▶ Coherence makes visible the links and connections that lead to deep learning.

▶ When things are coherent, all levels of the organization can learn together and enhance each other, enabling greater change for improvement.

How I Do It

▶ Develop a shared language and understandings.

▶ Promote work across levels in the organization.

▶ Relate all actions back to the focus (how does this fit with what we are trying to do?).

▶ Look for how things link together, and make this explicit.

▶ Use conceptual and theoretical frameworks to express how things fit together.

▶ Test new ideas against the agreed frameworks for coherence.

Key Challenges for Me

▶ Seeing the links between actual actions and theories of action to determine the degree of coherence

▶ Holding on to the idea of "focused and deep" when new avenues open up in the work

▶ Supporting leaders to avoid distractions and competing demands in order to create coherence

▶ Realizing that building coherence is an ongoing challenge

What I Should Notice

▶ To what extent is there shared language and understanding about what is being worked on? Across the school? Across the district?

▶ How clearly can people articulate the focus and the reasons for the activities being undertaken?

▶ Are new initiatives explicitly linked to the main focus or are they ad hoc?

Available for download at https://resources.corwin.com/LeadingPowerfulPL

Building Coherence

What: Description of the Concept

Schools and school districts are very busy places that strive to meet a range of goals and objectives. This can lead to fragmentation of effort and lack of clear direction. People have only a certain amount of time and energy: Making sure it is used well is critical to the effective facilitation and leadership of learning. Building coherence describes the intention to align goals, activities, and outcomes in a school or district in order to maximize the effectiveness of our facilitation work. Building coherence increases the power and impact of facilitation work.

> *"[Coherence] means that schools develop a set of interrelated instructional programs for students and staff that are guided by a common framework . . . and pursued over a sustained period."*
>
> (Lai, Timperley, & McNaughton, 2010, p. 58)

What: Description of the Deliberate Act of Facilitation

Building coherence involves helping leaders and teachers to link what they are doing and thinking to their purpose and theory for improvement (Lai et al., 2010). Simply put, it demands aligning thinking and actions to improve valued student outcomes.

As facilitators of learning, we are working to align the activity that is happening at all levels of the school system with the purposes and frameworks developed by educators—district leaders, school leaders, and teachers. Sometimes it is easier for those who are less embedded in the context to see where misalignment is occurring. In these situations we have an opportunity to help build coherence by asking questions and giving reminders about overarching purposes and theories. For example, if activity is aligned, from the principal's office to the classroom, then energy will be directed toward the change you have identified as a team, and results will be more readily achieved. Keeping the main thing the main thing is essential.

Why It Matters

Building coherence links to the principles of human learning. The Organisation for Economic Co-operation and Development (OECD) identified "building horizontal connectedness" as one of its seven key principles of learning (Dumont, Istance, & Benavides, 2010). Horizontal connectedness refers to deliberately forming links among ideas and actions so learners can see how things are related to each other and to their context, leading to powerful and lasting learning. Having an overarching theoretical framework, in the form of a theory for improvement or "pathways driver diagram" (Bryk, Gomez, Grunow, & LeMahieu, 2015), helps

> *"When the focus is scattered, energy is dispersed and opportunities for collective learning are limited. Making a real and substantive difference requires that all of us pull together."*
>
> (Timperley et al., 2014, p. 11)

to contribute to the attainment of joint goals. Without an overall framework, actions will be isolated and their contributions to change will not be readily understood. When teachers and the school community can see where everything fits, there will be greater clarity and more energy for change. With coherence, all layers of the school and organizational context can learn together, enhancing the likelihood of deep change.

How I Do it

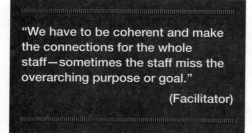

"We have to be coherent and make the connections for the whole staff—sometimes the staff miss the overarching purpose or goal."

(Facilitator)

Building coherence follows establishing a clear purpose. Having an articulated theory for improvement for the work is the basis for building coherence. Coherence across the overarching purposes and processes of change are both necessary components for effectiveness. To support a school or district in building coherence, facilitators need to look for links—between actions and purpose, between beliefs and actions, and between evidence and intentions—and make these explicit during interactions with administrators, leaders, and teachers. Deliberately building a shared vocabulary and deep understanding around the change process will help communication to be more coherent. This involves coming back constantly to the purpose of the work, asking "How does this fit in with our goal?" When new suggestions are made, or directions suggested, it is important to test these against the purpose and framework, asking everyone to think about how these ideas link to the agreed direction and in what ways they are coherent with the goal.

It is critical to build coherence across all levels in the school—with leadership, staff, families, and students if and as appropriate. Coherence is also important beyond the school and across the school district. The more "joined up" the work is, the more impact it will have.

Key Challenges for Me

"She linked the school's goals and the strategic plan and then kept asking me 'How are you doing? Don't forget the strategic plan!' She made the connections with what we were doing—it has to connect."

(Literacy leader speaking about the facilitator)

Building coherence can be difficult when there are many different possible directions and strong advocates for each of the different directions. This challenge can be compounded when there is significant turnover of teachers and leaders in an organization. Identifying priorities and sticking to them can be very challenging for school leaders who can see myriad issues that need to be addressed. Facilitators need to become skilled at seeing the links and recognizing when apparently disparate things might be conceptually linked. We also need to be able to articulate the links we see, or do not see, using language that is understood by the people with whom we are working. It can be difficult to stick with a narrowly focused, deep inquiry or work stream when new possibilities appear. As enthusiasm and buy-in builds, keeping everyone's activity coherent can be challenging.

What I Should Notice

As coherence builds in a school, language and understandings will become shared. Look for this in different parts of the school: Are some people on board and understanding the purpose while others are being left behind? When people are meeting to discuss the work, or to engage in PL related to the work, notice the extent to which people can articulate the focus and make their own links between what you and they are doing and the overall framework. If leaders and teachers are taking on the role of asking, "How does this fit in with our purpose?" then you can see that coherence is building amongst the staff. Notice the extent to which the framework and overarching purpose are used when thinking of new ideas and directions. Helping staff to have ownership of the underpinning ideas, and then prompting them to link their work back to this foundation, will help to build coherence.

Further Reading

Fullan, M., & Quinn, J. (2016). *Coherence: The right drivers in action for schools, districts, and systems.* Thousand Oaks, CA: Corwin.

Lai, M., Timperley, H., & McNaughton, S. (2010). Theories for improvement and sustainability. In H. Timperley & J. Parr (Eds.), *Weaving evidence, inquiry and standards to build better schools.* Wellington: New Zealand Council for Educational Research Press.

Vignette 3a: Building Coherence

F In a scheduled monthly catch-up with a principal, Fran learns that the principal's school is signing up for a new PL program: Action Assessment. Fran is concerned because the school has been focusing on engaging learners, and this seems like a new direction.

Working to align programs and build a coherent picture	*Fran:* That sounds like a really interesting program. One of the things we've been working on is to make sure everything links together so the teachers don't get confused about different ideas. So I'd like to explore with you how you see this new program fits with your previous work on engaging learners.
	Principal: Well, my vice-principal went along to the information session. It seems to be about having in-the-moment assessment and getting teachers using more formative assessment in their classrooms. I think we need that.
Relating back to the focus	*Fran:* Hmm. Yeah. Formative assessment is certainly something that can make a big difference to learning. How do you see this fitting in with what we are doing at the moment?
	Principal: I kind of thought that we were nearly done with that, like we'd need to move on, keep moving.
	Fran: I was looking at some of the information from the teachers, and I'm not sure the teachers have gone as far as they can in terms of engaging learners. There still seems to be a lot of concern and a bit of confusion, maybe? *Principal:* Yeah, I guess. This just seems like a great opportunity.
Looking for links	*Fran:* Well, maybe there's a link between what the program offers and what you've identified the school needs. Let's have a closer look at what they do and see if it lines up with what you need. We spent lots of time working that out. It's kind of been a touchstone for us.
Testing for new ideas	*Principal:* Yeah, I agree with that. I guess we need to use our focus to decide if this program will get us there or not.

Vignette 3b: Building Coherence

 Mateo is leading a professional learning community (PLC) meeting with his department. They are trying to talk about problem solving and what they should be teaching about it in Grade 8. Mateo realizes that they are talking at cross-purposes, because not everyone means the same thing by *problem solving*. There are also some issues with timing: Some teachers feel that problem solving takes too long and that they can't meet their commitments to covering the curriculum if they use a problem-solving approach. Other teachers point out that if they don't use problem solving, they are not addressing the Common Core State Standards.

(Continued)

(Continued)

	Mateo: So, let's just stop for a moment and take a breath. I think we've got a kind of miscommunication thing here, because I'm not sure we all mean the same thing by problem solving.
Developing shared language	**David:** I think you're right. I mean, I'm relying on the Common Core idea, but I think Maria means like, just word problems, or routine kind of "math test" stuff.
	Maria: But that's what they have to do, ultimately, like it doesn't matter how creative they are or whatever. In the end it's those kinds of problems we have to teach them how to do. And if we let them experiment, it just takes too long.
	David: I agree that we don't seem to have enough time between tests to really get into some of this stuff.
Aligning across the levels to build coherence	**Mateo:** Well, we could change that. We could have fewer tests, or bigger gaps between the—if that lined up with what we think is important—but let's come back to what we mean by problem solving. I think it would helpful to make a shared definition because it will highlight some of these differences and we can work through them.
	David: Okay, but where do we start? Other people must have looked at this before.
Using conceptual frameworks	**Mateo:** I think we need to build it together, for us—but we could start from the Common Core, or we could start from what's in our textbooks.
	Maria: Maybe look at both and see what's the same or different.

Creating Commitment and Taking Action

DAF **#4**

What It Is

▶ Create a commitment to productive action.

▶ Promote collaborative accountability to ensure a commitment to productive action.

▶ Be aware of how perceptions of risk can hamper deliberate action.

▶ Ensure that leaders and teachers have the will as well as the necessary skills and knowledge to take action.

Why It Matters

▶ Commitment and action are essential for change, without which there will be limited impact on student outcomes.

▶ Underlying all DAFs is the necessity to create commitment and take action.

▶ Creating commitment and taking action are central to a social justice agenda.

▶ A culture of collaborative accountability is necessary to ensure improvement occurs and is sustained.

How I Do It

▶ Commit to both notice and take action.

▶ Make sure there is a shared understanding of why actions are being taken.

▶ Co-construct commitment to action by being clear about next steps.

▶ Take a strengths-based approach to engaging others in taking action.

▶ Check on and hold people accountable for agreed actions.

▶ Pay attention to those who aren't on board.

▶ Acknowledge uncertainty, and help people manage it.

Key Challenges for Me

▶ Getting people started

▶ Engaging the reluctant

▶ Ensuring agreed actions are undertaken through systems of collaborative accountability

▶ Taking action when not everyone is on board

What I Should Notice

▶ Who is and isn't on board?

▶ Is there a shared understanding of what actions will be taken and why?

▶ Are people clear about the next steps for which they are responsible, and are they the right actions?

▶ Is there a culture of accountability for agreed actions?

 Available for download at https://resources.corwin.com/LeadingPowerfulPL

Creating Commitment and Taking Action

What: Description of the Concept

Creating commitment and taking action are essential to effective facilitation. One of the central challenges of any PL initiative is to ensure that learning and improvement actually occur, and one of the ways facilitators can do this is by creating commitment to change on the part of school leaders and teachers and promoting collective accountability for taking action. Facilitators need to create a commitment to productive action as a result of PL and development. Taking action is an essential component of, for example, inquiry processes, and, once the impact of the agreed changes has been observed and measured, the new practices should be embedded into the routines of the school, ensuring changed practices as a result of PL.

What: Description of the Deliberate Act of Facilitation

Facilitation conversations can create momentum and generate good discussion about change and potential courses of action. An important part of effective facilitation is getting learning and improvement happening.

Schools are busy places with a great deal happening at any one time, so it is easy for the actions agreed on during a PL session to be later pushed to the bottom of the priority list. Some of the barriers to taking action can be removed by ensuring that leaders commit to creating the conditions in which the agreed actions can take place—perhaps by providing resources or arranging release time. Creating a culture of collective accountability in which teachers and leaders hold one another accountable for taking action will help to promote a sustainable commitment to action beyond the term of the PL contract.

Teachers' and leaders' perceptions of risk may hamper deliberate action. Perceptions of risk can be a primary cause of nonengagement in PL and development, so recognizing and addressing these feelings of risk is an important step in creating commitment and promoting action arising from the PL (Twyford, Le Fevre, & Timperley, 2017).

It is important to ensure that leaders and teachers have the will to take action, but it is also essential that they have the necessary skills and knowledge. Using an agreed model of inquiry will ensure that the requisite skills and knowledge aligned to the proposed actions for change are identified and targeted in the PL.

Why It Matters

PL and development research consistently demonstrates that PL rarely leads to changed practices, and one of the primary causes of this lack of change is a simple failure to take action. Creating commitment and taking action are essential for change, without which there will be no impact on student outcomes. While it can be difficult to trace a causal relationship between our actions as facilitators and a shift in student outcomes, there is no doubt that action is essential for change.

"One of my key things is how do I get action, how do I get commitment to action that matters, that will have high value?"

(Facilitator)

Creating commitment and taking action are central to promoting a social justice agenda. Creating commitment to engage in PL and take action as a result of it goes hand in hand with a desire to create improved outcomes and reduce disparity in achievement for all students. Different contexts will offer possibilities for different ways to create commitment and take action. Common to all, however, is the importance of having a commitment to social justice as a facilitator and creating this commitment in those with whom you work. An effective way to create commitment to a social justice agenda and promote productive action in pursuit of this agenda is to link the PL to the school's agreed valued student outcomes.

Facilitators have an important role in ensuring that teachers and leaders hold themselves and each other accountable for completing agreed actions. This can sometimes mean ensuring actions are completed between visits or working sessions with the facilitator. Commitment to productive change persists beyond the term of the PL contract when maintained by a culture of collective accountability. This kind of accountability is a core characteristic of effective communities of practice.

How I Do It

We can create commitment to action by first committing both to notice and to take action ourselves. The next step is to co-construct commitment to action within schools: be clear about what the next steps are, establish who is responsible for what, and clarify how the leader and teachers will hold themselves accountable for the promised actions. It is also important to make sure there is an explicit shared understanding of why actions are being taken so that there is consistency and effective implementation of the agreed changes.

Taking a strengths-based approach to engaging others in taking action will help them to build from areas in which they are most effective in order to improve practice. Checking regularly on the outcomes of action will ensure that the leaders and teachers are on the right path. It will allow for changes to be made in a timely manner, if necessary, and for successes to be celebrated and used to drive further action and change. Success is acknowledged by research on PL to be a great source of ongoing motivation and commitment to action.

> *Being clear about next steps and who is responsible for what is important, but making sure there is a shared understanding of why actions are being taken is equally important.*

It is also important to pay attention to those who aren't on board and to discover the reasons why. It may be that perceptions of risk have not been addressed, or it may be that the necessary conditions for action, such as the provision of release time, are not in place. Sometimes a lack of engagement at the leadership level prevents other educators within the school from proceeding with their agreed actions. Acknowledging uncertainty and helping people manage it is part of this process.

Key Challenges for Me

Getting people started is one of the most important stages of PL but also one of the most difficult. It is much more comfortable to stay in the information-gathering stages of inquiry. It can be particularly challenging to engage the reluctant, but inquiring into this reluctance, acknowledging uncertainty, and recognizing perceptions of risk will help to uncover and address the sources of reluctance.

A consistent challenge in most contracts that involve outside facilitators is ensuring that agreed-upon actions are completed between facilitator visits. There are any number of distractions in schools and plenty of valid reasons why educators have been too busy to tackle their agreed-upon tasks. Holding people accountable is difficult, but promoting collaborative practices can lead to a culture of collective accountability in which teachers and leaders hold themselves and each other accountable.

Taking action when not everyone is on board is also challenging but Timperley and colleagues (2014) assert that it is important to get started nonetheless. Observable success may be the motivation that some reluctant team members need to get them engaged and involved: "Engaging in a process that addresses genuine learner-related challenges builds the commitment that is required over the long haul" (Timperley et al., 2014, p. 6).

What I Should Notice

> "I'm thinking there's another bit that you haven't done and . . . you know you should have done it but you haven't done it . . . you know some of this stuff but there's not an action there, so that's filed away."
>
> (Facilitator)

One of the first things to notice is who is and isn't committed to the PL and the agreed actions. A lack of engagement may be associated with unacknowledged perceptions of risk (Twyford et al., 2017). It is particularly important for us to notice if those who are not committed are responsible for creating the conditions to allow others to complete their agreed tasks, as this will hamper action at all levels.

Another thing to notice is whether there is clarity and a shared understanding of the actions to be taken and why and whether leaders and teachers are clear about the next steps for which they are responsible. A shared understanding will help promote commitment, and understanding the reasons for change will ensure the right actions are being taken. Clear allocation of responsibilities can help to create optimum conditions for action and foster a culture of accountability for agreed actions, as all team members are clear on their own and others' responsibilities.

Further Reading

Timperley, H., Kaser, L., & Halbert, J. (2014). *A framework for transforming learning in schools: Innovation and the spiral of inquiry.* Melbourne, Australia: Centre for Strategic Education.

Twyford, K., Le Fevre, D., & Timperley, H. (2017). The influence of risk and uncertainty on teachers' responses to professional learning and development. *Journal of Professional Capital and Community, 2,* 86–100. Retrieved from https://doi.org/10.1108/JPCC-10-2016-0028

Vignette 4a: Creating Commitment and Taking Action

P Penny is meeting with some of the teacher leaders in her school. They've been talking about the students' literacy data, which shows that the students start just below state averages, but each successive year they get further and further from the state average until by Grade 6 they are down on the fifteenth percentile. They are discussing what they might do in the face of these results.

Having a shared understanding of why	**Deb:** Well, to be honest, I don't know how much we can do about this. I mean, only so much of this is about school—it's about home, and family, and the community, and stuff. It's not just us. I mean, we work pretty hard at this stuff and we're just getting nowhere.
	Penny: Yeah, there's a lot of things impacting this. What do you think, Mike? **Mike:** Well, I know what Deb means, but I think in the upper grades there are things we could be doing differently too. Like, I'm not sure how much time we are actually spending teaching reading, for example. If we really looked at it, how much time do the kids spend being taught how to read?
Having a shared understanding of why	**Deb:** In the lower grades it's more about getting them to sit down with a book. They're easily distracted and hard to keep on task. I think sometimes maybe teachers opt for a free choice time or something instead. **Penny:** I think we need to work out together why we have these results. These ideas are a great start. Should we open up the discussion to the whole staff? **Deb:** I think as a first step we need to sort out why we think it's happening and then hear their ideas.

Defining action with next steps	**Mike:** Good idea. It would be good to feel we are all on the same page before we take it to others. I think some of them might be quite defensive about their practice, so we'll need to be kind of open to that.
Having a strengths-based approach	**Penny:** It is tough stuff. Okay, so we'll work as a group to think about why these results are so low, and then we'll work out a way to involve the rest of the staff in similar thinking. You know, one thing I noticed was that some of the children are making rapid progress, even though they are starting from a low base, so there's some good practice out there. **Mike:** We could look at what's happening there and how that might help the school generally.

Vignette 4b: Creating Commitment and Taking Action

P Liam is working with a literacy inquiry group in an elementary school. They've spent the past few months collecting and analyzing student data on reading and writing as well as students' opinions of their literacy learning. It's become clear that reading comprehension is a problem—both assessments and students' comments suggest this.

Checking outcomes of action	**Liam:** So last time I was here we talked a bit about where to go next, about what you were going to do with this information. We decided to share it with the wider staff. How did that go?
	Ben: Well, it's been so busy with the parent nights and sports day that we haven't had a chance to do that. **Liam:** Hmm. Have we moved forward in other ways?
Defining actions with next steps	**Sarah:** To be honest, it's been a bit on the back burner because so much else is happening and . . . well, I don't know, we just don't get to it. **Liam:** So maybe we need to make more of a formal plan, with some names and dates by tasks, and I can help with getting some more time for you.
Paying attention to those not on board	**Timo:** Yeah, okay, but I'm still not sure that this is the right thing to do. That spelling program we looked at would be a whole lot easier to implement than all this talking about comprehension. We could buy the books, give them to everyone. It's nice and clear and will be easy for people to do.
	Liam: So, you're not sure that reading comprehension is the right focus? **Timo:** It's more that reading comprehension is going to be really hard to work on, like it's big and I'm not sure that I understand it, let alone can lead it. I mean, how do you improve reading comprehension, like day to day?
Acknowledging uncertainty and helping manage it	**Liam:** That's a really important point. Thanks, Timo, I'm sure lots of people feel the same. Reading comprehension is a really big area. Maybe we need to zone in a bit on some parts of it, to help people learn how to improve it, but also what it is made up of.

Branch 2. Knowledge and Inquiry

The second cluster of DAFs is closely related to the roots of an evaluative inquiry stance and valuing and using deep conceptual knowledge. If an evaluative inquiry stance and valuing and using deep conceptual knowledge underpin your facilitation practice, then you need to work using a collaborative inquiry process, drawing on your own and others' knowledge to address your purpose.

These three DAFs explain critical aspects of working with an evaluative stance through an inquiry process. Thinking about knowledge together with inquiry reminds us of the multiple types of knowledge that are needed (knowledge of content, of pedagogy, of leadership, of inquiry processes, of students, and so on) and also that all participants in inquiry processes hold valuable knowledge to be shared. Part of our role as facilitators is to mobilize the knowledge that the people we are working with already hold. Another important aspect of this is to recognize that our worldview is only one of many and that knowledge, and how it is held and shared, differs among cultures.

The three DAFs centered on knowledge and inquiry are as follows:

1. Deepening knowledge
2. Using evidence critically
3. Using focused and deep collaborative inquiry

Deepening Knowledge

DAF #5

What It Is

▶ Build knowledge of relevant content areas that brings together the what, the how, and the why.

▶ Organize new knowledge into conceptual constructs that are connected and flexible as well as able to be retrieved when needed.

▶ Create the desire to learn new knowledge and ways of doing things to solve persistent problems in teaching and learning.

▶ Help teachers to understand others' worldviews, particularly those from cultures different from one's own.

▶ Build knowledge of students' identities, languages, cultures, and family practices.

Why It Matters

▶ Adaptive expertise and responsiveness are fueled by deep knowledge that is organized into conceptual frameworks.

▶ New knowledge that challenges existing beliefs forms the basis of new practice.

▶ Knowledge developed to solve teaching and learning problems is more likely to be applied than knowledge developed in the absence of such problems.

▶ New knowledge needs to be personalized and applied in a teacher's own contexts.

▶ Ways of knowing are central to identity and culture and are often embodied in language.

How I Do It

▶ Use frameworks and larger concepts from research to deepen new knowledge and anchor it to powerful ideas.

▶ Unpack the meaning of these frameworks by making direct connections to teachers' own

contexts and the problems of practice they want to solve.

▶ Jointly construct new knowledge with teachers so they understand its relevance.

▶ Create a space where sharing knowledge and narratives of practice are valued and link these to new knowledge of practice.

▶ Build knowledge of multicultural and bicultural practice and learners from cultures other than your own.

Key Challenges for Me

▶ Integrating the what, how, and why of new knowledge in teachers' own contexts

▶ Linking educators' narrative and problems of practice to conceptual frameworks in the moment, when it is needed

▶ Creating the desire for teachers to find out new ways of doing things and overcoming the desire to tell them what you know out of context

▶ Working with plural knowledge bases in multicultural or multilingual settings

▶ Knowing your own strengths and weaknesses as a facilitator and being prepared to ask for help if you need it

What I Should Notice

▶ What are the compelling problems of practice that teachers are experiencing?

▶ Are teachers making the links between the conceptual frameworks and their problems of practice? Can they see the relevance?

▶ Have I created the desire for teachers to know new ways of doing things?

▶ Can teachers identify how to apply new knowledge they have built through working together?

online resources   Available for download at https://resources.corwin.com/LeadingPowerfulPL

Deepening Knowledge

What: Description of the Concept

> *"To establish a firm foundation for improved student outcomes, teachers must integrate their knowledge about the curriculum, and about how to teach it effectively and how to assess whether students have learned it."*
>
> (Timperley, 2008, p. 11)

Knowledge is essential to PL (Bransford, Brown, & Cocking, 2000). Without knowledge (of curriculum content, of teaching, of how people learn, of culture, of change processes, of leadership), leaders and teachers will struggle to make effective changes to practice. New knowledge often forms the basis of change by helping leaders and teachers to understand what or how to do things differently.

No one doubts the importance of building new knowledge in PL. Rather, the issue is what kind of knowledge because this is such a contested space. Leadership and teaching are practices, so knowledge of and for practice is a good starting point. This is often depicted as the what and the how.

Theoretical or conceptual knowledge is sometimes seen as less relevant, but unless teachers understand the why (e.g., why new practices are likely to be more effective than existing practice), we argue that teaching becomes deprofessionalized, and this is the antithesis of adaptive expertise. In addition, if underlying theoretical ideas are well understood, new knowledge is more likely to be transferrable from one context to another (different curriculum areas, different students). Pellegrino and Hilton (2012) refer to deep knowledge as transferrable knowledge.

Complicating the issue of *what* knowledge is, the question of *whose* knowledge should be valued. We have as a starting point the increasing body of research knowledge that over time and contexts has demonstrated advances in student learning. However, teachers have difficulty applying this generic knowledge to their own contexts because knowledge is individually and socially constructed, so one of the tasks of those involved in PL is to help teachers to translate how this typically generic knowledge can be applied in their particular teaching and learning situations.

Knowledge building cannot be seen as a one-way process, from facilitator to teacher, but rather needs to be co-constructed between them. A one-way flow of information rarely results in sustained changes to practice because it does not engage with or address teachers' current knowledge and beliefs or the problems they need to solve in their particular contexts.

Work on knowledge building needs to acknowledge that there are different ways to know. This understanding is particularly important in all bicultural and multicultural contexts because knowledge is linked to identity and forms part of the unique features that make up that identity, whether teachers' or students' (Mead, 2012). Failing to respect or bypassing this knowledge can lead to feelings of being misunderstood or rejection of new knowledge.

What: Description of the Deliberate Act of Facilitation

> *"Observations followed by professional discussion are really powerful, helping to build that content knowledge and that shared understanding of what we're looking for."*
>
> (Facilitator)

As facilitators we are aiming to build knowledge that is flexible, conceptually organized for retrieval when it is needed, and able to be transferred to new situations. In order to create this kind of knowledge, it needs to be integrated into conceptual frameworks. The teaching of writing, for example, does not exist outside a teachers' beliefs about what is valued in writing, the curriculum, or discipline demands as well as how these particular students learn to write and how best to teach them. If a teacher's existing conceptual framework is sound, then the new knowledge may be a refinement of that framework. On the other hand, if a teacher's existing framework is problematic (e.g., these students can't learn to write in ways required of this discipline), then the new knowledge needs to interrupt and challenge current conceptual frameworks. This is a much more challenging exercise.

Teachers are more likely to be motivated to learn new ways of doing things if they understand how they might address the immediate teaching and learning challenges they are currently facing in their learning environments. The new knowledge is more likely to be taken on board and applied than more abstract knowledge for which teachers cannot perceive an immediate application. So constantly making these links is essential.

An important characteristic of knowledge building in the metaphor of the tree is learning together in context; engaging different worldviews, cultures, and identities; and respecting different ways of knowing. When teachers are able to do this with each other, they are more likely to respect and engage the worldviews of their students. The values underpinning building new knowledge are closely linked to the root of valuing and using deep conceptual knowledge, and there is considerable crossover.

Why It Matters

Knowledge of leading, teaching, and learning is fundamental to adaptive expertise. It is not possible to be responsive to in-the-moment challenges without having deep knowledge on which to draw. Knowledge that is able to be retrieved when needed must be organized into conceptual frameworks so teachers can analyze students' learning challenges and draw on appropriate knowledge to meet those challenges. Discrete pieces of knowledge not organized in this

> *"Learning environments are knowledge centered as well as learner centered."*
>
> (Bransford et al., 2000, p. 194)

way are typically forgotten. Bransford and colleagues (2000) explain that teacher PL needs to take place in a knowledge-centered environment, where teachers think deeply about subject matter and its role in their learning and the learning of their students.

New knowledge that challenges existing beliefs runs the risk of being rejected by teachers, but if it is accepted as valid and perceived as likely to be helpful in solving immediate teaching and learning problems, it forms the basis for new professional practice (Timperley, Wilson, Barrar, & Fung, 2007). The process of constantly linking new knowledge to existing beliefs and the challenges of practice helps teachers to personalize and internalize new knowledge as they apply it. Knowledge in leadership and teaching cannot be separated from practice because it is through practice that understanding is deepened.

How I Do It

Research frameworks and larger concepts can be used as organizers to build the specifics of what, how, and why of practice in a particular practice context. It is often difficult for teachers to connect a big idea from research to the challenges of teaching their students in their context. This constant integration of big ideas and the specifics of practice is essential for the knowledge to become part of an individual teacher's own conceptual framework, retrieved and applied when needed.

During this process, meaning is unpacked, connections are made, and learning is deepened. The process is particularly powerful if teachers can see how new ways of doing this assist with solving those persistent teaching and learning challenges they have been experiencing for some time.

> "I'm going to use their own conceptual understanding that they've got within their group and flesh it out from there. It's always coming back to what they know isn't it? They've got their prior knowledge; how do I build on that and extend on that?"
>
> (Facilitator)

Knowledge needs to be built with leaders and teachers, rather than delivered, in order to respect prior knowledge, to open up the possibility of reciprocal learning, and to be responsive to teachers' learning needs (Timperley et al., 2007). New knowledge is always interpreted in terms of existing knowledge and beliefs, not separately from it. It is important, therefore, for facilitators to engage with those beliefs and jointly construct new knowledge for practice together. Through the exchange and engagement of existing beliefs and ideas, teachers are more likely to perceive the relevance and value of new knowledge while feeling their existing knowledge and understandings are respected.

This does not mean that, at times, providing knowledge about specific aspects of teaching and learning is inappropriate. These are times when teachers or leaders request input, when learning needs have been identified through an inquiry process, and when there is a clear need for just-in-time information that can be used to solve the learning challenge the teachers are grappling with. What does not work is facilitators telling teachers things that the teachers do not necessarily want to know.

Through engaging with different beliefs and views of the world, facilitators help to model how teachers may engage with different beliefs and cultures of the students. It may be important, however, to go beyond this respect of others' views and specifically deepen knowledge of multicultural or bicultural practices that explicitly engages with students' worldviews and identities.

Key Challenges for Me

Building integrated knowledge of and for practice that links wider conceptual frameworks with narratives of specific problems of practice is challenging. This involves facilitators listening closely to what teachers are saying, drawing out, and illustrating the links as they speak.

Many teachers are reluctant to admit gaps in their knowledge because they are coming from a routine expertise rather than adaptive expertise framing of what it means to be professional. Richard Elmore (2004) claims that one of the strongest social norms in schools is that everyone is expected to pretend they are equally effective in what they do, even when they feel unprepared to do it. This belief is the antithesis of adaptive expertise where we all accept that our knowledge is sufficient to solve the complex problems of teaching and learning. We all need to learn together to create new approaches to doing things.

The acquisition of new knowledge needs to be driven by an urgency to solve persistent problems. Creating this desire to learn and solve problems in teachers who have been practicing for years is often challenging. The skill is to demonstrate how new knowledge about doing things differently will make a difference to their learners.

There are many types of knowledge, much of it contested, and many different worldviews. Things that seem acceptable or obvious from one perspective may not be in a different framework. Working in multicultural settings with plural knowledge bases can be challenging and requires an openness to learning orientation from us as facilitators.

Acknowledging our own deficiencies can be challenging. In knowledge building we need to be fallible and prepared to ask for help from others when we need to and to admit when we don't know.

What I Should Notice

One of the most important aspects to notice is whether teachers are actively engaging in building new knowledge through evidence of changes in practice. Passive engagement is unlikely to make much of a difference. Active engagement in learning without changing practice is also unlikely to make a difference (Le Fevre, 2010). Active engagement is evident when teachers demonstrate their processing of new information by verbalizing the links they are making to their own contexts, building on each other's ideas, and following up with narratives of success about progress in student learning to share with others.

Further Reading

Le Fevre, D. M. (2010). Changing TACK: Talking about change knowledge for professional learning. In H. S. Timperley & J. Parr (Eds.), *Weaving evidence, inquiry and standards to build better schools* (pp. 71–91). Wellington: New Zealand Council for Educational Research Press.

Pellegrino, J., & Hilton, M. (Eds.). (2012). *Education for life and work: Developing transferable knowledge and skills in the 21st century.* Washington, DC: The National Academies Press.

Vignette 5a: Deepening Knowledge

P Liam is working with a group of teachers who are looking at their teaching of reading. The teachers' fifth-grade students are struggling with making inferences from what they read. They can read the words on the page, but they can't seem to access the meanings behind the words.

Beginning from the teachers' knowledge and their context	*Liam:* So, tell me a bit about what is happening with the students' reading. What are you worried about?
	Avril: Well, it's a long-term problem that we've never managed to work out. The children are good enough at decoding the words, reading aloud, that kind of thing. Like, they can read the words, but then once you start asking them about how a character might feel, or what they think was really going on, they just look at you as if to say "I read it. Was I supposed to be finding that out?"
	Darcy: And they aren't really getting what they need from their reading because they are not building that next level of comprehension. They can't do anything with it.
Creating drive to learn and solve problems	*Liam:* Sounds like you've got a clear idea of where the problem is. It's a tricky one too. How do we get children to read *beyond* a text? What do they need to know? It's hard.
	Becky: Yeah, it is, and a lot of the time the strategies you get told don't really work for our students. A lot of the activities we are given are meant to build inferencing, but it's like these students don't even realize that inferencing is part of reading. They can't do the activities if they don't get the point. I can get them busy doing book reviews or character posters or feelings graphs or something, but they aren't linking back to the text.
Deepening knowledge with teachers, not telling	*Liam:* Is there anything you are doing that seems to work? At least a bit?
	Ava: I've been trying close reading study of pieces from books that are really relatable for the students and going through highlighting with them and labeling the things that the author is doing—the clues, kind of—and then listing together the hidden things or guesses we can make based on what's there. I've been being really explicit about what the task is—getting the meaning out.
Teachers building on each other's knowledge	*Becky:* That sounds interesting. I've been coming at it from a writing point of view. Children find it hard to put themselves in their readers' shoes while they are writing. It's a bridge too far sometimes—maybe working from a piece of existing writing would work better.
Organizing knowledge into conceptual frameworks	*Liam:* These are really useful ideas, and they make me think about something that might be helpful here for us—researchers sometimes distinguish between different types of inferencing, and the different types can be helpful in thinking about how we might teach it.
Linking the context to the framework	*Liam goes on to explain different types of inferencing.*

Vignette 5b: Deepening Knowledge

 Penny is worried about the well-being of a number of the students in her school. These students seem uncomfortable and unhappy at school. They often behave in ways that challenge their teachers. Penny thinks this is getting in the way of their learning. She is thinking about introducing a health and well-being curriculum that might support the students in understanding themselves as learners and being more settled and confident. She is talking about this idea with her vice-principal, David.

	Penny: I just think they've got low self-esteem. They aren't valuing themselves as learners. They just undermine their own learning all the time with their behavior. It's clear they aren't happy.
	David: Yeah, you know I'm not sure about that.
	Penny: Really? It's pretty clear, I think. They aren't engaged. They just don't seem to want to be here. We need to build them up so they want to engage.
Recognizing plural worldviews	**David:** From what I see they are engaged—just not with a lot of the stuff we think they should be engaged in. They play sports, dance, have lots of music happening. They're engaged in church groups and youth groups out there in the community, helping their families. Maybe they see school as different from the other things they do.
Recognizing plural worldviews	**Penny:** But what about their academic work? If we don't help them make progress in schoolwork, they are really going to have limited opportunities later. But I see what you mean. I guess coming from outside this community I'm maybe not seeing things they do outside of school. What am I missing?
Recognizing need for new knowledge	**David:** You're right about the academic work. These kids deserve the best we can give them. But I'm not sure that the behavior is about them. It might be about us. What do we know about how they see school? About how their families see school?
Asking for help when you need it	**Penny:** Seems we need to know more here. I've had visits from some community leaders and parents since I arrived. I didn't really ask them much, just thanked them for coming in. Maybe I could reach out to them again, ask them to help us learn.
Creating space for knowledge building about identity, language and culture **Co-constructing with others**	**David:** Our kids are a resource too. Let's try talking with them in a systematic way about what they need.

Using Evidence Critically

What It Is

▶ Build an evaluative mindset to use evidence to identify what is working well and what needs to change.

▶ Help teachers to select and collect a range of relevant evidence about student progress to answer important questions.

▶ Help leaders and teachers to collect relevant evidence of changes in teaching practice to explain student progress.

▶ Develop skills in analyzing, interpreting, and using evidence through a critical lens to inform all levels of decision-making.

▶ Create an awareness that the evidence selected and how it is interpreted may be influenced by biases and assumptions that have implications for social justice.

Why It Matters

▶ Engagement in PL does not guarantee improvement in outcomes for students; these improvements need to be assessed with evidence.

▶ Standardized tests are usually insufficient to make ongoing judgments of improvements in student learning; a range of more relevant evidence is needed.

▶ Changes in student progress coupled with evidence of changes in teaching practice unpacks teaching or learning links.

▶ Evidence of improvements in student learning can be a motivating tool for getting teachers on board and keeping them on track.

▶ The evidence selected and how it is interpreted is rarely neutral and requires careful unpacking for potential biases and assumptions.

How I Do It

▶ Use evidence of student learning profiles as the reason to engage in PL and to check ongoing progress.

▶ Help teachers to identify the evidence they value as indicators of progress and to collect it systematically throughout the process.

▶ Work with teachers to collect evidence of changes in teaching practice so that they can see the links to improvement (or lack of it) in student learning.

▶ Make sure that evidence is used to make decisions and drive change rather than just collected, collated, and analyzed or used to justify current approaches.

▶ Ensure that interpretation of evidence is a collaborative process that deliberately invites alternative viewpoints.

▶ Keep asking, "What is your evidence for that?" in response to untested assumptions.

Key Challenges for Me

▶ Creating the mindset that using evidence is central to the development of adaptive expertise

▶ Helping teachers to identify a range of valid evidence that they value sufficiently to pay attention to

▶ Getting caught in the busywork of change and not taking the time to test the efficacy of that change

▶ Dealing with contradictions in evidence and prioritizing many directions that could be pursued

▶ Understanding the purpose and limitations of tools for evidence gathering and using these appropriately

▶ Finding the collective story in the evidence that promotes rather than undermines social justice

What I Should Notice

▶ How is evidence being used currently—critically, uncritically, or not at all?

▶ What are teachers' past experiences of and current attitudes to the use of evidence?

▶ Who owns it? How is it used? Is it facilitating the development of adaptive expertise?

online resources

Available for download at https://resources.corwin.com/LeadingPowerfulPL

Using Evidence Critically

What: Description of the Concept

"While test results and data systems provide information about achievement, we need to dig much deeper to find out what is happening for learners in other key areas of learning and engagement."

(Timperley et al., 2014, p. 9)

A central tenet of adaptive expertise is using evidence to understand the impact of teaching practice on student outcomes. This involves checking whether changes made through PL are making enough of a difference to these outcomes. Particular attention needs to be paid to the impact on those students currently not well served by our schools. The burgeoning field of improvement science has the use of this kind of evidence at its core (see, for example, Bryk et al., 2015; Timperley et al., 2014). Bryk et al. (2015) even go as far as saying that we cannot improve at scale what we cannot measure. This means that we need to start by having evidence of what is happening for student learners at the beginning of the process of change and to have this evidence form the reason to engage in new PL. Also needed throughout is evidence of the changes made by teachers in their practice and evidence of the resulting outcomes for students on an ongoing basis. When teachers seek evidence of their impact, they are thinking evaluatively and developing adaptive expertise.

What counts as relevant evidence is often contested. Evidence is not neutral and has inbuilt assumptions about what is important to measure and how best to measure it. From this shaky starting point, even more important are the potential biases and assumptions brought to the interpretation process. What does it all mean? Do low test scores for a group of students indicate that they have low ability? Do these low scores mean they have had insufficient opportunities to learn through inadequate teaching? Is the test itself irrelevant? There are many other possibilities, and to treat any one as an obvious answer is the antithesis of engaging with evidence critically. Teachers often reject evidence because they have problems with at least some of these assumptions, and at times their concerns are justified. It is essential, therefore, that the participating teachers are involved in decisions about the evidence collected and what it all means. This unpacking of meaning is enhanced when multiple perspectives are brought to the process. Evidence cannot serve the purposes of improvement science if it is considered invalid and unreliable by those expected to be responsive to it and make changes to their practice as a result.

What: Description of the Deliberate Act of Facilitation

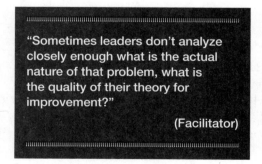

"Sometimes leaders don't analyze closely enough what is the actual nature of that problem, what is the quality of their theory for improvement?"

(Facilitator)

Using evidence critically involves the collection, collation, analysis, and use of evidence through a critical lens. The central purpose of evidence in a change process is to identify what is working well and should be retained, what needs to change, and whether those changes are leading to desired improvement in student outcomes. There are several parts to the process where facilitation is central. Schools and leaders may need help with identifying what evidence they have and what to collect, how to draw their evidence together to build a picture of what is happening for their learners, how to analyze particular types of evidence to yield useful information, and how to then bring the evidence to bear on finding a focus and driving change. The main purpose is to establish a way of working where everyone involved is thinking evaluatively with the use of evidence becoming second nature and an accepted part of making judgments and decisions.

At all stages of this process a critical lens is needed: Who does this evidence serve and why? What might be missing? Whose experience might not be accurately represented by this evidence? How are we capturing the experience of all learners in evidence gathering and analysis?

It is rare that a single source of evidence provides sufficient information about what is working well and what needs to change. Two, equally problematic extremes are often adopted. One is the use of a single standardized test, but this is rarely adequate to give a nuanced picture of what is happening for learners or their teachers. The other is a reliance on teachers' anecdotes and hunches. Finding the middle ground of rich evidence that can be systematically collected, analyzed, and used as well as perceived as valid by those expected to be responsive to it is a major facilitation challenge.

A frequent gap in the evidence is changes that are occurring to teaching practice as a result of participation in PL. Collecting this kind of evidence is typically even more fraught. Self-report is unreliable, as are observations— particularly when their purpose is perceived as one of checking up on a teacher rather than promoting PL.

Why It Matters

Change is central to improvement but does not guarantee it, so it is essential to gather evidence to find out if change is indeed leading to improvement. Usually these kinds of evaluative judgments involve the use of multiple sources of evidence about student outcomes and changes in teaching practice. While these sources need to be kept manageable, it is important to collect evidence about what is valued rather than to value what is easily collected.

> *"Evaluative capability requires using evidence throughout teaching and learning cycles."*
>
> (Timperley et al., 2010, p. 31)

It is challenging enough to collect valid evidence of changes in student learning, but it is even more challenging to collect parallel evidence about changes in teaching practice. Unless evidence of these changes is systematically collected, it is very difficult to explain accelerated (or no improvement) in student outcomes and to decide what should be retained and what should be changed. Unpacking evidence of these teaching-learning links develops evaluative thinking and is central to the development of responsiveness to students and adaptive expertise.

One of the benefits of collecting evidence is that accelerated progress in student learning can be highly motivating for teachers to come on board and to stay on track with the PL and change process. Without the systematic collection of evidence, such progress is often missed. When teachers have a clear and nuanced view of the kinds of progress they want their students to make, and are helped to systematically observe these small changes, then responsiveness to evidence becomes a daily activity rather than an event at the end of a period of time. This process is the realization of responsiveness through the development of adaptive expertise.

> "We need to be collecting evidence continually to avoid wasting too much time on things that might not have an impact."
>
> (Facilitator)

How I Do It

Using a systematic, evidence-informed inquiry approach will embed the use of evidence in the change process. Inquiry approaches begin by asking what is going on for our learners and how we know. Once the focus of the change process and the desired outcomes are decided, evidence is used to check regularly if the change is making enough of a difference to learners in terms of the desired outcomes. The more teachers are involved in investigating what is going on for their learners and deciding what evidence would be indicative of progress, the more likely they will perceive it as valid and be responsive to it.

The same process applies to gathering evidence of changes in teaching practice. The more teachers are involved in deciding what evidence would be indicative of change and how they could collect it collaboratively and systematically from an inquiry mindset, the more they are likely to use it. Evidence that is decided by others, collected by others, and imposed on teachers does not lead to it being used. Rather, it is usually ignored or rejected as invalid.

Usually much more time is spent on identifying and collecting evidence than on its interpretation (Earl & Timperley, 2016). Yet it is the interpretation process that leads to its use. Multiple and sometimes conflicting interpretations are possible, yet the process is often left to individuals to decide what it means. Collaborative processes that respect multiple perspectives are nowhere as important as in this interpretation process and are at the center of using evidence critically.

As facilitators we can encourage this critical use of evidence by asking questions and suggesting that the participating teachers turn to evidence to back up the claims they are making. We also need to model critical thinking about evidence by questioning and reflecting out loud about patterns or links we see being made between the evidence and inferences or assumptions we are making. Being respectfully challenging by asking "What is your evidence for that?," for example, models a way of thinking and working that is driven by an evidence-informed inquiry mindset.

Key Challenges for Me

Using evidence critically involves skills and knowledge that leaders and teachers may not yet have and may not perceive that they need. Asking them to gather evidence to answer the question "What is going on for their learners?" may be a new experience because of previous reliance on anecdotes and assumptions. As a facilitator, this may also be a new and challenging experience and the exercise is best undertaken as a joint inquiry by all those involved, with the adequacy and meaning of the evidence discussed regularly and further investigations decided. The process needs to be ongoing and iterative.

Deciding on a focus from the evidence gathered can be difficult because the evidence may indicate many different possibilities. If gathered from a genuine inquiry stance, the information can be challenging and sometimes unwieldy. Careful facilitation is needed to help choose the most important direction at this time, and to face the, at times, confronting facts that the evidence presents. An ever-present challenge is to prevent evidence being used to reinforce deficit thinking or other negative assumptions about learners.

Significant change always involves a great deal of energy and work. Yet significant change is usually needed to improve outcomes for learners. It is easy to get distracted by doing the work rather than checking if it is having the desired impact.

What I Should Notice

Understanding how teachers and leaders currently use evidence, particularly student progress and achievement, can be a good starting point. This will give an indication of their current skills in using evidence and, more importantly, their attitudes to it. Negative experiences where evidence has been used to make personal evaluations and judgments about them as professionals is a very different starting point than positive situations where evidence has been used for learning purposes. Trust in the inquiry and learning purpose and the development of adaptive expertise will take time to build.

Where evidence is used, it is important to take note whether the participating teachers have experience in using a range of evidence sources and whether they can draw reasonable conclusions from different types of evidence. To what extent is reference to sources of evidence becoming a habit?

Listen to the professional conversations, and note if they are evidence informed, based on untested assumptions and anecdotes and whether these conversations are focused on advancing the learning of our most vulnerable students.

Further Reading

Earl, L., & Timperley, H. (2016). *Embedding evaluative thinking as an essential component of successful innovation* (Seminar Series 257). Melbourne, Australia: Centre for Strategic Education.

Robinson, V. M. J. (2018). *Reduce change to increase improvement.* Thousand Oaks, CA: Corwin.

Vignette 6a: Using Evidence Critically

 Mateo and his teachers are looking at the results of a recent algebra assessment in a department meeting. In the past they have given the assessment, recorded the results by class, and moved on to the next unit of work. Mateo has suggested that they meet to look at what happened in the assessment and to see if there is anything they need to follow up on.

Helping teachers to collect relevant data and develop skills to analyze it	*Mateo:* So, thanks for coming along with your algebra test results. I know we haven't done this before so it's a bit different, but I made a spreadsheet that has got all the students on it so we can look across without thinking about yours and mine. I think we can see all the students as ours really. You've got your own lists to kind of compare with, but my chart is anonymized. Okay?
	David: Yeah, sure. This is kind of interesting. You know, overall they weren't as bad as I thought. It's easy to focus on the ones who haven't got it when you look at your own list.
Interpreting data through a critical lens	*Maria:* There's a bunch of them though, there, that group—they are way off the bottom in terms of total score, and there's a few of them there. I wonder who they are, like do they have something in common?
	Elisa: They probably all come from my class. I feel like I got nowhere with algebra this time.
Analyzing evidence so it can be interpreted critically	*Mateo:* That's not very likely, Elisa, but it is worth asking if the students have something in common in case it's a group of kids we are missing the mark with. On this version I've labeled each data point with gender, ethnicity, and first language.
	Thomas: That doesn't make it much clearer. They're quite a mix.
	Maria: But many more boys really. And English language learners (ELLs)—it almost looks like most of the male language learners in the grade are in that group.
Having alternative viewpoints in interpretation	*David:* But some of them are at the top too.
	Maria: Sure, but is there something going on here that we could do something about?
Recognizing that the evidence is not neutral **Thinking about assumptions that underpin interpretations**	*Elisa:* Could it be the test for those students? We asked a lot of word problems this time. They had to understand the relationships in English before they could put them into algebra—how many times more and stuff. Maybe this is not the best evidence of their algebra learning.
Having alternative viewpoints in interpretation	*Thomas:* Or maybe they are not getting it in class.
Selecting relevant evidence to understand student progress	*Elisa:* I wonder if they are all getting the same things wrong—I mean, we are working with totals here and we designed the assessment, so each question tested something important. What happens if we look at the data question by question?

Vignette 6b: Using Evidence Critically

L Liam is working with all the teachers in a small school, looking at their students' progress in writing. Teachers and parents have identified writing as an issue over a period of years.

	Fran: So, you've been looking at ways to give more in-the-moment or just-in-time feedback to students for a year now. How do you think it's going?
	Mandy: I think the students are more engaged and focused. I feel like that's the case in my classes and in my department at least. Enjoying it more, I guess, happier.
	Brady: Yeah, I'd say the children are happier, and so the teachers are too. Happy kids, happy teachers!
	Marilyn: But some people still aren't doing it really. I'm not sure how much real change there's been in some places. Maybe pockets of change—and I guess we are committed to it, so we've tried hard, but others, maybe not so much.
	Jorge: It's not easy. Maybe in some subjects, but physical education? Physics? I know some people have struggled. I'm not sure I do it every day.
Asking for evidence to justify assumptions and statements **Linking teacher change to student change**	**Fran:** Thank you for sharing those impressions with me. It sounds like maybe it depends where you are in the school how much change you think there has been. Let me ask you two things: First, what evidence do you have for the changes you describe? Second, has anything changed for the students? Do you have evidence of that?
	Jorge: Well, as part of the PL we had to gather some evidence from the students about what they thought. Most people have done that, but we haven't done anything with it at a school level—departments may have looked at it, but we haven't done an overview or anything. **Brady:** There's not much for the teachers though. I guess we've got some observations of each other, the ones we did in September.
	Mandy: That was before we made most of the changes.
Developing an evaluative mindset by asking for evidence **Helping leaders think about what evidence to collect about teacher practice**	**Fran:** I think evidence is really important here. It's quite easy to jump to conclusions based on one or two conversations or seeing a lesson. What kinds of evidence could we collect to help us with the teachers' practice changes? The student evidence sounds interesting, so we probably need to work out a way to make better use of that too.
	Brady: It's hard to know what we could collect. The in-the-moment stuff isn't in planning.
Helping leaders think about what evidence to collect about teacher practice	**Fran:** I could help you with some ideas that other schools have used if you like.

Using Focused and Deep Collaborative Inquiry

DAF
#7

What It Is

▶ Deep inquiry involves being genuinely curious about what is going on for learners and how to make a difference to their learning.

▶ It is deepened by using evidence systematically and critically throughout.

▶ Effective inquiry includes examining the ways in which educators are contributing to any issues and their underlying causes.

▶ Inquiry focused on one area with high impact deepens learning and promotes its transfer to other students or situations.

▶ Targeted new PL and action arises from the inquiry into what is going on for learners and how the educators are contributing.

▶ Inquiry is deepened through iterative cycles until student learning is accelerated and issues addressed.

Why It Matters

▶ Inquiry that is focused, deep, responsive to student challenges, and based on evidence is at the core of adaptive expertise.

▶ Focused inquiry is more manageable for teachers, has high leverage for change, and allows learning to be transferred.

▶ If change is to become a reality, inquiry must address current professional knowledge and practices.

▶ New knowledge and action are created through solving student learning and achievement challenges.

▶ Deep inquiry is motivating for teachers to make ongoing changes to their practices as they make a difference to student learning.

How I Do It

▶ Model curiosity, and hold a constant inquiry stance, including the use of evidence.

▶ Ensure that teacher inquiry is focused on what is happening for learners, and check with evidence if new learning and action is having an impact.

▶ Examine with teachers the ways in which they and other educators are contributing to the current situation.

▶ Encourage teachers to be open-minded about problems and solutions and the impact of their actions.

Key Challenges for Me

▶ Developing a common language that supports collaborative and co-constructed inquiry

▶ Ensuring inquiry is genuine and driven by curiosity, not just confirming existing beliefs

▶ Helping teachers to identify the practices that may be contributing to student learning issues

▶ Closely connecting the inquiry process to new PL

▶ Planning for transfer from the deep focus to other students or curriculum areas

▶ Promoting inquiry as a mindset and deepening the process through engagement in multiple cycles

What I Should Notice

▶ Is the inquiry process driven by curiosity, or do teachers think they already have the answers?

▶ What evidence is relevant to inquiry about what is going on for their learners?

▶ Is inquiry deep and focused or superficial and general?

▶ What assumptions about students and teaching do teachers bring that should be tested?

online
resources
Available for download at https://resources.corwin.com/LeadingPowerfulPL

Using Focused and Deep Collaborative Inquiry

What: Description of the Concept

Evidence-informed, systematic inquiry is one of the OECD's 21st century competencies (Pellegrino & Hilton, 2012), and it is at the very heart of adaptive expertise.

> *"The development of rigorous inquiry processes ensures that valuable professional learning time is not wasted, but rather focused on what needs to be learned to achieve better outcomes for students."*
>
> (Timperley, 2011, p. 128)

Le Fevre, Robinson, and Sinnema (2014) remind us that "the concept of inquiry is central to contemporary educational discussions of teacher and leader professional learning" (p. 883), but much of it is pseudo rather than genuine inquiry. The difference is the extent to which the inquiry "is characterized by openness to learning in contrast to resistance to new ideas or information, excessive certainty about one's own ideas, and unreflective rejection of other people's ideas" (p. 884).

A major conclusion of the best evidence synthesis on PL and development (Timperley et al., 2007) was that an inquiry approach to PL had far greater impact on changing teacher practice and a range of student outcomes than more traditional approaches to PL and development. This conclusion is strongly supported by subsequent analyses of effective professional development in high-performing countries (Jensen, Sonnemann, Roberts-Hull, & Hunter, 2016).

Inquiry is strengthened when facilitators are coinquirers with teachers into what is going on for learners and what needs to change to make a difference. The job of the facilitator, therefore, is to help others to develop a similar inquiry orientation and commitment to action.

What: Description of the Deliberate Act of Facilitation

Inquiry begins with a phase of scoping or scanning in order to assess what is going on for learners and to identify a focus that will make a real difference to students. The focus needs to be manageable for teachers and have evidence to support it. This last attribute associates it closely with the "Using evidence critically" DAF.

Focused and deep inquiry is always driven by the needs of students rather than what teachers or leaders perceive is important to them. It is easy to get distracted by "firefighting" the problems that schools present. Effective facilitation develops focused inquiries that begin with evidence of student outcomes and cut through the layers of the school system. Evidence of student needs drives the inquiry by providing a bottom line to return to as the inquiry progresses.

A central feature of deep inquiry is to identify how leaders and teachers are—usually inadvertently—contributing to what is happening for learners. If everything is kept as it always was, then not much is likely to change significantly for students. These kinds of issues may include school structures and processes, teacher knowledge, and their teaching practices. This process deepens the inquiry and identifies what needs to be addressed in order to change (e.g., restructuring of classes or the school day, building teacher knowledge and practice).

> "I find inquiry is like a metacognitive framework of 'is something working or not' . . . which leads us on to the next cycle of inquiry about where to [go] next."
>
> (Facilitator)

Building new leadership or teacher knowledge as the basis for changing practice becomes motivated by the process of finding out about what is going on for the student learners and how they, as professionals, may be contributing. Hence, the DAF "Deepening knowledge" is an integral part of the inquiry process because without new knowledge little is likely to change. Timperley et al. (2014) highlight the importance of this in their inquiry spiral: "This phase is critically important because better outcomes for learners are a result of teachers and leaders acquiring new skills that lead to new actions" (p. 14).

The next key stage of the inquiry process involves evaluating the impact of the new actions and changed practices arising from the new learning. We need to find out what happened as a result of chosen actions. It is this measurement of impact that will inform the next stages of the inquiry and establish whether or not the goals of the inquiry in terms of improved student outcomes are being met. It is important to persist in the inquiry process until the improvement goals are realized. This may involve several iterations of the process. Inquiry is not a single event. It is inherently cyclical and as such is constant, ongoing, and generative of further inquiry.

Inquiry is also a vital tool in promoting linguistic and cultural responsiveness (LCR) practices because LCR hinges on having and promoting a deep curiosity to understand what is happening for learners. What is more, it is important to use theories about LCR to support inquiry—scanning from an informed knowledge base and from multiple points of view. In this way inquiry both supports LCR and is informed by it.

Why It Matters

Inquiry is important because it is effective. Timperley et al. (2014) attest the following:

> It is through a disciplined approach to collaborative inquiry, resulting in new learning and new action, that educators, learners, their families and involved community members will gain the confidence, the insights, and the mindsets required to design new and powerful learning systems . . . It is well within the capacity of all schools to make dramatic changes. We have seen it happen in a wide range of complex and challenging situations across different countries where educators, learners and their communities construct new and more innovative learning environments together. (p. 4)

This effectiveness is only realized, however, if collaborative inquiry teams drive the process, feel in control of it, with the outcomes being the result of their collective efforts. Curiosity and inquiry cannot be mandated by others. Rather, facilitators can ask the questions, help with the collection of evidence, and model an inquiry mindset to promote curiosity throughout the process.

"Innovation floats on a sea of inquiry and . . . curiosity is a driver for change."

(Timperley et al., 2014, p. 4)

Deep inquiry involves surfacing beliefs to enable educators to identify, share, and critique the assumptions that underpin their leadership and teaching practices and how they may be contributing to learner outcomes. Some of these beliefs are likely to be getting in the way of students making greater progress. Through the sharing of beliefs, and the practices that may be contributing to the current situation, the inquiry process can prompt educators to challenge prior assumptions and broaden the possibilities for change (Le Fevre et al., 2014). Positive change for improvement will never be achieved unless educators first engage with their own often unrecognized and untested assumptions about their contribution to the current situation.

Deep and focused inquiry is motivating for teachers to engage and change practice and can lead to innovation. Timperley et al. (2014) insist that "creating the conditions in schools and learning settings where curiosity is encouraged, developed and sustained is essential to opening up thinking, changing practice and creating dramatically more innovative approaches to learning and teaching" (p. 4). Inquiry leads to the creation of new knowledge as leaders and teachers engage in new learning and try out new practices in order to address organizational and achievement challenges.

Iterative spirals of inquiry result in shifts in mindsets and lead to sustainable practices. The chances of sustained inquiry-driven practices continuing after the professional development contract ends are enhanced by identifying, with school leaders, aspects of inquiry that can be applied to new problems. Sustained improvement is more likely to occur if responsibility for change and the ownership of the inquiry process rest with the leaders and teachers in a school rather than professional development facilitators.

How I Do It

As facilitators, we can promote the use of focused and deep inquiry in schools first and foremost by modeling and holding a constant inquiry stance and by considering others and ourselves as learners. It is important to scan from the perspective of the students, particularly from an LCR point of view, and to ensure that the process becomes focused, deep, and informed by the evidence. It is important to remain open-minded about problems and solutions. The most common limitation on genuine inquiry is "solutionitis" (Bryk et al., 2015). This happens when the professionals jump to solutions without finding out what is really going on for learners and failing to ascertain how they are contributing to the situation.

Inquiry must be a collaborative process because it is too difficult for an individual to identify his or her own assumptions about learners and how they may be contributing to the situation. Deep inquiry needs challenging conversations and evidence to get to the essence of important issues.

Key Challenges for Me

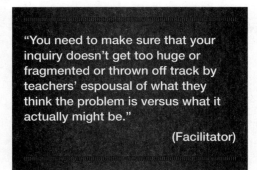

"You need to make sure that your inquiry doesn't get too huge or fragmented or thrown off track by teachers' espousal of what they think the problem is versus what it actually might be."

(Facilitator)

It may be difficult at the outset to develop a common language for inquiry, as some educators may not be accustomed to working collaboratively to pursue inquiry. It is challenging and risky for many people to engage in work that involves surfacing and challenging beliefs, particularly in a collaborative setting.

Another challenge is to ensure that inquiry results in action and that the impact of this action is measured. There is a fine line between jumping to solutions before understanding what is happening for learners and inquiring for prolonged periods of time without engaging in new PL of doing things differently.

Establishing inquiry as a mindset that addresses core teaching and learning issues, rather than an event, can be challenging. To achieve this mindset change leaders and teachers need to persist in cycles of inquiry until the improvement goals are met and then to move on to new inquiries. Too often completion of the process rather than a real improvement in student learning is considered success.

In addition, transfer and sustainability need to be built by facilitators. Ownership of the process and outcomes need to rest with the teachers and schools. To undertake the process without external help, they need the knowledge and mindsets to enact this ownership with skill.

What I Should Notice

Inquiry approaches to PL are successful only if the process is motivated by curiosity. Wanting to know what is happening for learners and what needs to change in educators' knowledge and practices is fundamental to its success. An important attribute to notice, therefore, is whether educators are genuinely driven by this curiosity or whether they believe they have the solutions before they start.

Gathering evidence is fundamental to finding out what is happening for learners and often serves to challenge educators' existing beliefs and assumptions. Noticing if conversations are informed by evidence or just someone's opinion is important. Are teachers open to testing their assumptions with evidence with the potential for them to be challenged?

Is the inquiry process sufficiently deep and focused to allow teachers to use evidence to assess whether they are making the desired difference, or is it so superficial and general that it is having little impact?

Further Reading

Jensen, B., Sonnemann, J., Roberts-Hull, K., & Hunter, A. (2016). *Beyond PD: Teacher professional learning in high-performing systems* (Australian ed.). Washington, DC: National Center on Education and the Economy.

Timperley, H., Kaser, L., & Halbert, J. (2014). *A framework for transforming learning in schools: Innovation and the spiral of inquiry.* Melbourne, Australia: Centre for Strategic Education.

Vignette 7a: Using Focused and Deep Collaborative Inquiry

L Liam is working with all the teachers in a small school looking at their students' progress in writing. Teachers and parents have identified writing as an issue over a period of years.

	Bailey: So, we know there's a lot of problems in writing at our school at the moment—from handwriting, spelling, grammar, whether or not they can punctuate, writing for different purposes, vocabulary. Students are bored with writing, disengaged—they hardly write anything! It's so hard to know where to even start.
Establishing curiosity and impact as two criteria for choosing where to start	**Liam:** It is. When there seems to be lots of issues, how do we decide where to start? I'd say two things. First, what puzzles you the most. Second, what would have the most impact on the children's writing if it improved?
	Sandra: You don't reckon we could have a go at all of it? I was thinking that we could take a topic each, kind of research it, find out what we should be doing and bring it back to the group, share ideas. It's all so linked that if we don't tackle all of it, it won't get fixed.
Focusing the inquiry **Keeping it narrow and deep** **Building curiosity about learners as a basis for inquiry**	**Liam:** I know what you mean. It certainly is all linked. But I think there's a risk that we could spread too thinly and end up confused and not improving things. Let's talk for a minute about the learners and their writing. What puzzles you about their low performance?
	Monica: For me, I have the youngest children. It's what happens after they leave me. They hit all their early benchmarks in writing—know their alphabet, basic words, can write a sentence with support. Then it seems to be all downhill. Why is that?
	Darren: In the upper grades I am really interested in the relationship between their oral language and their writing. If they just record the way they speak then it's not grammatical and it's hard to follow, but it's their genuine voice. When we try to shoehorn them into "proper English" they shut down, but they need to be able to write using proper English to get ahead in middle school. They are good at expressing themselves, just not good at formal writing.
	Monica: That is a problem for me too—the oral language. I guess what we write is so structured I don't let them explore much, so I avoid this issue.
	Sandra: Yeah, that is interesting. What role does writing play for them? Are they expressing themselves, or what?
Beginning to focus the inquiry by referring back to the evidence	**Liam:** Okay, so are we talking about how children can tell their own stories in writing? Might this help them produce more writing and engage more as a starting point? How does this link to the evidence we have about writing? Let's take a look at the samples you have.

Vignette 7b: Using Focused and Deep Collaborative Inquiry

Penny, her senior staff, and teachers have begun an inquiry into their learners' experience of school, trying to understand how they feel about the school and what could be done to improve it for them. They are having trouble getting helpful responses from the students, who frequently shrug and say they don't know when asked about how they'd like their school to be. Penny is talking to her vice-principal about ways forward.

	David: Well, we don't seem to be getting anywhere fast.
Using evidence to choose a focus **Trying to narrow down inquiry**	*Penny:* True. You know, I think it's because we've been too broad and too abstract. We ask them "What don't you like about school?" Where would they start to answer that question? And they might be afraid to tell us. After all, we are the school as far as they are concerned. I think we need to narrow down our inquiry and focus on the overall issue through a particular subject context. Reading seems to be a big concern. We have lots of evidence of slow progress and low achievement in reading. If we took reading, we could say "How do you think students learn to read best?" That's a more answerable question.
Having a narrower and deeper focus for transfer	*David:* Agreed. It also gives us a chance to ask about reading at home and reading at school. It gives the inquiry an anchor, but it's an anchor based in data. If we get some traction in reading it may spread to other areas.
Having genuine curiosity about learners **Choosing a high-impact inquiry focus**	*Penny:* And reading is high impact—improve reading, and we'd improve a lot of other things. We are curious about our students' experience of our school, but we need a focus to help us drill down and understand more.
Implicating educators' practice	*David:* It also makes our role clearer too. If we are talking about reading, we can talk about how our practice might need to change if that's what comes up.
Starting from evidence about learners	*Penny:* So, we've got evidence about reading progress from our benchmark tests. Let's begin with that, with all the staff, and see what questions and hunches we have about the students' reading. Then we need some more information from the students about how they experience learning to read. We'll need to get everyone on board with this.
Using iterative cycles of inquiry until improvement occurs **Having genuine curiosity about learners**	*David:* I think they'll be interested in the students' perceptions alongside the progress data. They care a lot about their kids! This builds on what we've been trying to do too.

Branch 3. Effective Learning Processes

The third cluster of DAFs describes the use of effective learning processes in adult, education, and problem-solving contexts. Working with adults, in complex settings on difficult problems, is not just about changing behavior or thinking. It is also about emotion. Often, as outsiders or leaders, we think we can see a simple solution to a challenge, but once we get started on the change, we find it is more fraught than we thought it would be. If we act as supporters and never challenge, we will not get the changes we need. If we challenge too much, we will lose the goodwill and motivation of those we are working with. These DAFs explore ways of working with educators with an awareness of the holistic nature of being human that respects the theories and beliefs, feelings, and values people hold.

We have identified five DAFs that leaders of learning can consider to help support and drive effective learning processes. They are as follows:

1. Surfacing and engaging theories and beliefs
2. Navigating perceptions of risk
3. Developing self-regulation
4. Providing appropriate support and challenge
5. Co-constructing learning

DAF #8

Surfacing and Engaging Theories and Beliefs

What It Is

▶ Seek to understand the constraints on own and others' actions.

▶ Understand that theories and beliefs can be aligned or misaligned with intended change.

▶ Be aware of theories and beliefs that are problematic (e.g., deficit theories).

▶ Be prepared to be courageous and take action when theories and beliefs get in the way of learning.

▶ Persist as beliefs may be entrenched, and people may not be aware of the beliefs that drive their actions.

Why It Matters

▶ Theories and beliefs drive actions consciously and subconsciously.

▶ Our theories and beliefs are connected to our personal and professional identities. Theories and beliefs are fundamental to how people learn, teach, facilitate, and lead.

▶ Theories and beliefs develop over long periods of time, are deeply held, and can be difficult to change.

▶ Theories and beliefs can change as a result of experiencing dissonance and from seeing students succeed.

How I Do It

▶ Be aware of how own theories and beliefs are impacting on situation.

▶ Make own and others' theories and beliefs visible.

▶ Provide a culture of support and safety for changing theories and beliefs.

▶ Provide opportunities for people to experience dissonance.

▶ Engage in talk about both cognitive and emotional aspects of changing theories and beliefs.

▶ Help identify and make outcomes of problematic theories and beliefs explicit.

Key Challenges for Me

▶ Changing theories and beliefs that can feel risky and confronting for those involved

▶ Understanding that what people actually believe may be different from what they say they believe

▶ Navigating own and others' emotional responses to have theories and beliefs challenged

▶ Supporting people to share their actual theories and beliefs

What I Should Notice

▶ What are people saying and doing?

▶ What do their actions say about their underlying theories and beliefs?

▶ What happens when people experience disconfirming evidence about their beliefs?

▶ How does cultural positioning influence theories and beliefs?

▶ How valid are the assumptions being made?

---

online resources

Available for download at https://resources.corwin.com/LeadingPowerfulPL

Surfacing and Engaging Theories and Beliefs

What: Description of the Concept

To surface something is to be aware of its existence, and to engage with something is to understand the nature of it, to consider its impact, and to question its validity. Surfacing and engaging theories and beliefs is not easy work, but it is important as the theories and beliefs one holds influence the way one acts.

People are often unaware of the underlying theories and beliefs that drive their actions (Argyris & Schön, 1974). These theories and beliefs have a powerful impact and can be difficult to change; they also make change difficult. Theories and beliefs influence what people learn from professional development and how they engage with change for improvement. If one's theories and beliefs do not align with an intended change for improvement, then change is unlikely to occur (Robinson, 2018).

"Theories and beliefs are important to understand because they drive a person's actions."

(Richardson, 1996)

Sometimes people hold theories and beliefs that are problematic and contradictory to evidence about effective practice. Engaging problematic theories and beliefs demands more than recognizing them; it also involves actively challenging and working to change them. This is challenging because people hold espoused theories or "theories of talk and they also hold theories of action or theories of walk" (Robinson, 2018), and these are often not aligned.

What: Description of the Deliberate Act of Facilitation

Surfacing and engaging theories and beliefs is an important DAF. It is important to be able to identify the underlying theories and beliefs that drive one's actions as a facilitator and to be able to change these when they are problematic. Effective facilitators also have the important role of supporting those with whom they work to do this.

This can be delicate work as our theories and beliefs are connected to personal and professional identities.

Surfacing and engaging theories and beliefs for the purpose of improving practice demands that people hold "a general epistemological outlook of fallibilism, a recognition that we are sometimes mistaken" (Hare, 2009, p. 38). This requires being willing to acknowledge that our own ideas and the ideas of others may be incomplete or inaccurate.

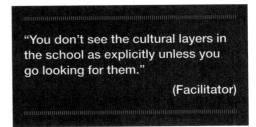

"You don't see the cultural layers in the school as explicitly unless you go looking for them."

(Facilitator)

Why It Matters

In order to bring about learning for improvement in education, it is necessary to surface and engage the understandings, theories, and beliefs people hold and challenge these when necessary. Theories and beliefs about effective practice can be varied, entrenched, and difficult to change (Bransford et al., 2000). Theories and beliefs are often developed over long periods of time, and often people are not even aware of the theories and beliefs that drive their actions (Argyris & Schön, 1974). Efforts to change existing theories and beliefs are confounded by the fact that people have a natural tendency to interpret new information through their existing belief systems (Bransford et al., 2000).

It is necessary to challenge and change problematic underlying theories and beliefs to enable educational improvement.

Ignoring teachers' beliefs is not an option as "by-passing teachers' existing theories . . . can lead to the rejection of the new practice that is based on alternative theories" (Timperley et al., 2007, p. 145). We rarely accept new or alternative theories without convincing evidence that they are either worthwhile or that there exists incontestable evidence against the existing belief (Coburn, 2001; Timperley & Robinson, 2001). Timperley and Robinson (2001) found that teachers' existing schema or beliefs did not change when there was insufficient "salience of the discrepant data to result in schema revision" (p. 297).

We know that change is not sustained without changes in our theories and beliefs, but there is mixed evidence as to whether change in practice or change in beliefs comes first. While some researchers found changes in beliefs preceded changes in practice (Richardson, 1996), others found that positive student learning results from changed teacher practices subsequently influenced teachers' beliefs (Guskey, 1986; Levin & Wadmany, 2006), while Timperley and Robinson (2001) suggest a less delineated and more iterative process.

Surfacing and engaging one's own and others' theories and beliefs is an important and DAF to promote LCR practice in schools. The development of LCR practice can sometimes be an area in which educators from the "majority culture" feel insecure about their own knowledge base. One of the greatest challenges for educators is the need to overturn rather than recycle systemic power imbalances. In this way, schools and classrooms become institutions that are concerned with notions of social justice and equity not only within the schools themselves but also throughout wider society. What happens in schools should not just be about the representation and celebration of cultural diversity but about helping "teachers envision alternative power arrangements in the process of schooling" (Sleeter & Montecinos, 1999, p. 125).

How I Do It

Talking about our own and others' theories and beliefs is essential for change and therefore needs to be a deliberate act. This involves investigating the thinking behind teachers' and leaders' practices. We also need to make our thinking about the problematic beliefs visible and publicly check with others for the accuracy of our own thinking. The ladder of inference (Robinson & Lai, 2006) is a powerful tool to help people check the validity of assumptions and claims about the world.

> "This work has made me realize that I now realize I need to be more active in surfacing thinking and beliefs about the linguistic cultural side of things."
>
> (Facilitator)

Theories and beliefs can be hard to change, and the ladder of inference can create dissonance or uncover disconfirming evidence to convince us of the need to change. Some beliefs may need to be further challenged.

An existing culture of support and safety makes it easier to surface and engage others' beliefs and theories that might undermine intended changes in practice. It is also important to be aware of our own theories and beliefs—especially our cultural positioning—so that we notice the impact of our practices on others.

We also can introduce and talk about how beliefs and theories drive what we think, do, and feel. This raised awareness creates an opportunity to talk about the process of changing beliefs and the involvement of cognition and emotion and that it takes time.

Key Challenges for Me

Key challenges for facilitators when surfacing and engaging theories and beliefs are often connected to the emotional responses we have when our theories and beliefs are different from those expected. This can make the work feel confrontational and create a feeling of risk for ourselves as we engage in "why we think the way we do." This is particularly evident when engaging race-based beliefs as they are deep seated and difficult to engage. However, with courage and planning it can and needs to be done for real change to occur. When carried out respectfully, relationships can be strengthened rather than damaged through the process.

People do not always share their underlying theories and beliefs, and when they do, there may be contradictions between their stated theories and beliefs and their actions. Time is often limited, and it can be tempting to bypass people beliefs in an attempt to get to a quick solution. However, because actions are driven by the theories people hold, "the target of change is not actions but the theories in use that sustain them" (Robinson, 2018, p. 19).

Another key challenge is to deliberately engage in surfacing and engaging beliefs, knowing that this is required for change. It can seem simpler and much less challenging for us to provide the answers.

What I Should Notice

It can be important to notice whether there is an existing school culture of safety to talk about underlying beliefs or if people are hesitant to share them. Why might this be? Have I deliberately engaged with beliefs or have I avoided doing so?

When deliberately surfacing and engaging beliefs it is important to listen for the underlying assumptions that inform people's actions and practices whilst also checking for how these espoused theories (talk theories) align with their actions (walk theories). For example, a person's race-based espoused beliefs may not align with the way they are acting.

Further Reading

Richardson, V. (1996). The role of attitudes and beliefs in learning to teach. In J. Sikula (Ed.), *Handbook of research on teacher education* (2nd ed., pp. 102–119). New York, NY: Macmillan.

Robinson, V. M. J. (2018). *Reduce change to increase improvement*. Thousand Oaks, CA: Corwin.

Vignette 8a: Surfacing and Engaging Theories and Beliefs

 Mateo is talking to his department about making changes to the way they approach teaching ratios and proportional reasoning. He is keen to use challenging problems to stimulate the students to struggle with the mathematical ideas and get them to work in collaborative groups. Some of his colleagues are not keen on this idea. Mateo wants to explore why.

Creating an opportunity to talk about theories and beliefs	*Mateo:* We've all had a look at the reading I suggested last week—the one about challenging problems. I'm eager to hear what you think. Might an approach like this work with our students?
	Thomas: It's interesting, sure, and it has appeal because of the math involved, but I think it's too time consuming. It will take forever to get through the curriculum if we do this.
	Elisa: I've tried something like this a couple of times. Once was really successful, the students were right into it, but like Thomas says, if we did that all the time we'd be so far behind we'd never catch up.
	Thomas: It seems pretty pointless to me to have them struggling too. What does that do to their confidence and attitude? Math is orderly, and making it disorderly seems unnecessary to me.
Making theories and beliefs visible	*Mateo:* Tell me some more about that—about math being orderly.
	Thomas: It's a set of rules and relationships that students have to master. It's organized and clear—that's the benefit of it. To help students learn math, we have to guide them through the steps. Sure, use problem solving for those who get it quickly, or at the end of a section of work, but starting with problem solving isn't going to help.
Making theories and beliefs visible **Understanding that beliefs can be misaligned with intended changes**	*Mateo:* I see. So, this approach doesn't fit with your underlying concept of what math is—and how it's best learned.
	Thomas: Exactly, I can't see how starting from problem solving is a good idea.

Vignette 8b: Surfacing and Engaging Theories and Beliefs

 Fran is helping a team at a junior high school with its system of reporting to parents. She has recognized some underlying assumptions about parents and students that are underpinning the school's choices about reporting. Fran wants to try and get these assumptions surfaced where they can be discussed and examined.

Creating an opportunity to talk about theories and beliefs	**Fran:** While you've been talking, I've made a few notes to try and pull out the key things you are saying. Let me put them up on the whiteboard here so we can all see them. • There is little interest from parents in students' progress. • We only hear from parents when there's a problem, usually a social one rather than an academic one. • Students hide their results from parents because they are scared of the consequences. • Not many parents in this area believe in education and support their child's learning.
	Bella: That looks about it—also the students don't want to be involved in reporting to their parents.
	Fran: I'll add that; it's an interesting point. I'd like to have a look together at these key things, have a look behind them and think about why we perceive that this is what is happening.
	Tom: It is what is happening.
Making theories and beliefs visible	**Fran:** Sure, let's take the first one then. You have parent-teacher conference afternoons where parents can make appointments to come and see the teachers and talk about their child's progress. You close the school to free up the teachers, but the parents don't come. This shows little interest from parents in students' progress.
	Tom: They can't even be bothered to come once a semester. And we spend hours preparing to talk to them.
	Bella: Some of them don't even reply to the invitation. Silence.
Making theories and beliefs visible	**Fran:** So, your theory about why they don't come is that they can't be bothered or are ignoring the invitation?
	Tom: Yeah, something like that—not respecting what we can offer them.
Understanding that beliefs can be misaligned with intended changes **Being prepared to take action when theories and beliefs get in the way of learning**	**Fran:** It's good to have that clear. I'll write it next to the statement about lack of interest. Thinking back to what you've described—not replying, not coming, and also thinking about how the parent-teacher conferences have been organized to date. What could be some alternative explanations? I wonder, for example, if the parents might not be available then because of child care issues. Let's see what we can come up with, and then we can figure out how to check our thinking.

Navigating Perceptions of Risk

DAF
#9

What It Is

▶ Emotion and feelings of vulnerability may be expected responses to new learning.

▶ Perceptions of risk are personal, dynamic, and multifaceted.

▶ Risk is an inherent part of change that involves uncertainty and vulnerability, and it is as important as cognition when considering responses to change.

▶ Risk involves thinking about the quality of relationships, the school and wider culture, and level of knowledge and confidence.

▶ Risk involves vulnerability, which can be positive (open and prepared to take risks) or negative (protective and unwilling to take risks).

Why It Matters

▶ People's willingness to engage with change can be reduced by reducing perceptions of risk.

▶ Perceptions of risk are changeable.

▶ Learning is reduced when the perceived risk is high.

▶ Nonengagement may relate to perceived risk rather than resistance.

▶ Leaders and facilitators can reduce perceptions of risk.

How I Do It

▶ Engage in talk about risk and change.

▶ Identify and reduce unnecessary uncertainty in the context.

▶ Consider own and others' impact, and share responsibility for learning.

▶ Deliberately build knowledge and confidence in others.

▶ Provide a culture of support and safety for learning and risk taking.

▶ Promote new learning as possibly uncomfortable.

▶ Develop learning-focused relationships of trust and respect.

Key Challenges for Me

▶ Not making assumptions about others' actions

▶ Acknowledging and navigating own perceived risk

▶ Noticing beliefs that ignore or contest risk in learning

▶ Challenging beliefs that view emotion as a weakness and nonengagement as willful resistance

▶ Navigating own and others' emotional responses

What I Should Notice

▶ How do people frame their own and others' emotional responses?

▶ What is the quality of relationships? Do they include mutual trust, respect, empathy, and support? Are people willing to ask for help?

▶ What are the gaps in teacher knowledge, and how big are they?

▶ Is there evidence of a supportive culture?

online resources

Available for download at https://resources.corwin.com/LeadingPowerfulPL

Navigating Perceptions of Risk

What: Description of the Concept

People are generally thought to have a conservative impulse (Marris, 1986), preferring the status quo over change to something unfamiliar. This may be because change demands intentional effort and may be accompanied by feelings of uncertainty and emotional responses including feelings of vulnerability. Indeed, perceptions of risk are an inherent and inevitable aspect of change, as change involves creating a degree of uncertainty about the processes and outcomes for those effected by the change. People can experience the feeling of losing something that is familiar (Ponticell, 2003) and have a sense of uncertainty when they are engaged with change. Perceptions of risk are mental constructions based on a person's judgment of the "uncertainty about and severity of the events (or outcomes) of an activity with respect to something that humans value" (Aven & Renn, 2009, p. 6). As such they

> "[Risk is defined as] uncertainty about and severity of the events (or outcomes) of an activity with respect to something that humans' value."
>
> (Aven & Renn, 2009, p. 6)

involve both ones' emotion and cognition. Perceptions of risk are personal, based on multiple factors including those from past and current experiences and contexts as well as uncertainty toward the future. Perceptions of risk are complex.

An individual's perceived confidence and competence in their knowledge and skills to be successful in what they are expected to do in the future also contributes to teachers' perceptions of risk, as does perceived failure in a previous event (Twyford, 2016). In this study, the teachers with lower confidence in their knowledge experienced increased feelings of vulnerability toward forthcoming events. These feelings can impact either negatively or positively on individuals. On the one hand, feelings of vulnerability can lead to unwillingness, insecurity, and self-protective actions, while on the other hand, vulnerability accompanied by relationships of mutual trust and respect can encourage a willingness to engage and take risks in learning new practices.

Perceptions of risk when engaging in PL for change are thought to be common. The majority of teachers involved in a PL initiative "experienced perceptions of risk, albeit at different intensitives" (Twyford et al., 2017, p. 91). Facilitators may also feel perceptions of risk in carrying out their work. Aspects of facilitators' work that influenced perceived risk revealed in our research are potential threats to credibility, especially given the public nature of the work; the continual pressure to facilitate improvement; and challenging others' beliefs and practices, especially in a way that leads to learning and change.

Although perceptions of risk are highly personal, they are impacted by the organizational culture; the quality of interpersonal relationships, particularly in relation to trust; and what others say and do or do not do. It is easier to take risks in a culture that supports mistakes, with someone we trust, and when the amount of new learning is perceived as attainable rather than overwhelming. This makes perceptions of risk dynamic and therefore challenging to predict, notice, and understand.

What: Description of the Deliberate Act of Facilitation

Navigating perceptions of risk starts with being aware that the teachers and leaders with whom facilitators work may perceive uncertainty and risk in changing their practice. Next, it requires taking notice of teachers' and leaders' responses, being prepared to consider perceived risk as a contributing factor, and then taking deliberate action to reduce the uncertainty or perceived risk. This is not easy as different individuals may respond differently to the same context and expectations of change. While negative emotional responses and reluctance to engage in the PL are readily observable indicators of perceived risk, other risk-related actions such as being overprepared or highly cautious and anxious about what is observed and who does or does not ask for help may also be indicative of an individual's perceptions of risk.

Being alert for and recognizing perceptions of risk as a response to new learning and change requires a mental shift from framing emotion and nonengagement as evidence of resistance (Twyford, 2016). Perceptions of risk are multifaceted and as a result we need to consider what contributes to the levels of uncertainty surrounding the PL, such as the quality of the relationships between teachers and leaders (and us), the level of knowledge and confidence of individuals, and the organizational culture in terms of how risk-taking actions are supported and responded to.

Perceptions of risk occur systemically across each layer of participants in PL, so, first and foremost, an awareness of the impact of our own and then others' perceptions of risk is necessary for effective facilitation. Perceptions of risk are further exacerbated by the specific PL context. The sensitive and sometimes political nature of working to develop LCR practice can evoke perceptions of risk that, if ignored, can interrupt the capacity for people to change and improve practice. Facilitators have an important role in navigating their own and others' perceptions of risk.

Why It Matters

Perceptions of risk impact people's willingness and capacity to learn and as such they can be a "significant roadblock to engaging in educational change" (Le Fevre, 2014, p. 6). Teachers with high perceptions of risk, especially if unrecognized or unacknowledged, are likely to avoid or resist engaging in change. Perceptions of risk impact the type of actions individuals take, especially the level of risk that they take when getting under way and trying new practices.

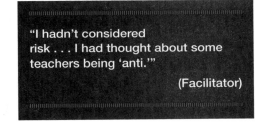

"I hadn't considered risk . . . I had thought about some teachers being 'anti.'"

(Facilitator)

Perceptions of risk are further exacerbated if our practice is exposed to others and we place our "confidence and perceived competence on the line" (Hargreaves, 1998, p. 324). It is important, therefore, to recognize and understand how perceptions of risk are formed, who and what mediates their formation, and how to deliberately support teachers who may be experiencing them in order to improve both their PL and student outcomes.

Leader, teacher, and facilitator data from our research revealed that when greater risk is perceived, participants' willingness to engage in a new practice was perceived to be less. This inverse relationship between risk and willingness was consistent across factors and participants and supports the theory that risk is an important concept to which to attend in educational change. While teachers may understand and agree with a practice in principle, if they perceive these practices as too high a risk to engage with, they will likely avoid doing so (Le Fevre, 2014).

How I Do It

Fundamental to navigating perceptions or risk is to be aware of the role of perceptions of risk and to make this transparent to those with whom you work. In addition there are some specific actions that can be taken to reduce perceptions of risk. Perceptions of risk reduce with increased confidence in one's knowledge. The development of relevant knowledge and skills is also a critical component of what leaders and facilitators can do to reduce perceptions of risk and increase the engagement of teachers in PL for improvement. Knowledge reduces unknowns and informs new ways of working that increase confidence to act.

"It is important to empathize with how they might feel if there is uncertainty about where the PL is heading ."

(Facilitator)

A supportive environment for risk taking includes making risks transparent and building and modeling relationships of trust to work beyond one's comfort zone, where all participants are genuinely learners and where learning is shared. It is an environment where people feel safe to have a go or say I don't know. Learning-focused relationships, where leaders and facilitators are learning with and supporting teachers, provide opportunities for building greater trust and a sense of shared vulnerability, which in turn increase willingness to engage. As a facilitator it is also important to promote new learning as potentially uncomfortable.

Showing empathy, trust, and respect toward others, as in the values of being open to learning, contributes to the building and maintaining of quality relationships. All interactions, including not taking action, have an impact on trust in relationships. This involves looking beyond any emotional responses to inquire into the support that individuals may need to take risks. Do not assume everyone has the same triggers or response to perceived risk. Recognize that teachers and leaders may not share their concerns with you, for example, by not asking for help or appearing invulnerable, and recognize emotional responses as possible indicators of perceived risk.

Key Challenges for Me

Perhaps the biggest challenge in navigating perceptions of risk is connected to the often-unexpected emotional outbursts and behaviors that appear to intentionally disrupt the PL. These responses can feel personal and can feel difficult not to react to and respond to emotionally. This requires that leaders and facilitators recognize the possibility of underlying perceived risk and understand what may contribute to the response. Reframing resistance as risk is a more agentic position to take.

Our own perceptions of risk can also create some challenges, especially when we are new to a school or working in areas where we are not confident in our knowledge and skills. Treating these situations as potentially risky can help us consider what we are uncertain about, then deliberately make decisions about the most appropriate action(s) to take.

What I Should Notice

Emotional responses are an expected response to learning-related events in schools and generally easy to notice but not often understood. It is important to check whether others label teachers' resistance to change a result of their emotional responses. The concern is that they may not inquire into this emotion and perpetuate incorrect beliefs regarding reasons for nonengagement in change.

The quality of relationships and a supportive culture contribute to the level of risk one is prepared to take. It is important to notice whether there are relationships of trust and respect, for example, shown through lesson observation outcomes being kept confidential and used for the purpose of supporting learning. A culture of trust is operating when it is acceptable for everyone to share mistakes as learners rather than only sharing successes. Leaders play an important role in being prepared to be vulnerable, so it is important to notice whether we default to wanting to appear invulnerable.

Further Reading

Le Fevre, D. M. (2014). Barriers to implementing pedagogical change: The role of teachers' perceptions of risk. *Teaching and Teacher Education, 38*, 56–64.

Twyford, K., Le Fevre, D., & Timperley, H. (2017). The influence of risk and uncertainty on teachers' responses to professional learning and development. *Journal of Professional Capital and Community, 2*, 86–100. Retrieved from https://doi.org/10.1108/JPCC-10-2016-0028

Vignette 9a: Navigating Perceptions of Risk

 Penny has begun a new program of observing teachers in their classrooms. She and the vice-principal are visiting each class to observe a science lesson and provide feedback to the teacher. Before they observe, they meet with the teacher to talk about what they are looking for in the lesson, giving teachers a chance to talk about their intentions in the lesson and to co-construct the area of focus for the observation. Penny is talking to Amy, one of the Grade 3 teachers, about her forthcoming observation.

	Amy: Which day are you coming? Next week is going to be fairly messy because of the sports day. It might not be a good week to come.
	Penny: Oh, I see. So you won't be teaching a science lesson next week?
	Amy: I will, but it might not be the same as it usually is. The lesson might be a bit shorter or simpler, to fit it all in.
Responding to individual's possible vulnerability	*Penny:* Uh-huh. I see. I do want to come at a time when you are comfortable, but it doesn't need to be a "special" lesson. I just want to see you at work with your class and provide some feedback that is useful to you for your development.
	Amy: I still don't really think next week is a good week because we won't be doing much science in the class. Actually, the following week is a bit tricky too as we have the school production stuff going on.
Thinking about emotion as well as cognition	*Penny:* I'm just wondering . . . I've noticed some people feel a bit worried about being observed. How do you feel about being observed?
	Amy: No one likes it, do they? I mean, yeah, it makes me stressed. I just feel like I must be doing something wrong or you wouldn't be coming in. You can say you're "just looking," but I worry that judgments might be made about my teaching. I don't want to look like a bad teacher.
Responding to individuals **Considering vulnerability and reducing uncertainty**	*Penny:* Hmm . . . I can understand why you might feel like that—I am the principal— but I'd like to talk some more about what I think we are doing here and how you can use it for yourself, have control over it. And what would make it less stressful for you. Is that okay?

Vignette 9b: Navigating Perceptions of Risk

 Sofia is talking to a principal from one of the schools in her district about their school participating in PL using an inquiry process. The principal has written in to Sofia to say that their school will not be participating in the PL because they are already using an inquiry process, and they do not want to learn more about it at this time. Sofia has looked at the PL plan for the school and can't see how inquiry fits in with the plan as it is written. She is wondering if there is something more behind the letter.

	Sofia: Thanks for your letter. I wanted to talk to you about it a bit more, just to understand more about what is going on.
	Mark: Sure, no problem. We've got a lot on, and we already use inquiry, so I just don't think it's a priority for us.
	Sofia: How have you used inquiry? I'm interested to know a bit more about that.
	Mark: Well, we've just dipped our toes in the water really. We've got teachers who are looking at various things, working with their teams.

Talking about risk	**Sofia:** It's usually quite a big change, implementing this way of working. It can sometimes feel a bit risky for people . . . it can make them feel unsure, maybe a little vulnerable.
	Mark: Yeah, which is why we haven't got far I guess. We're not ready to push ahead.
	Sofia: Hmm, not ready?
	Mark: To be honest, yeah, there's just a lot going on for my staff that means this extra stuff is a bit much, you know? They can't really deal with it.
Responding to emotion as well as cognition	**Sofia:** So, you feel like you are protecting them? They need a bit of support at the moment?
	Mark: They are telling me that they just can't make more changes, so I said I'd help them by trying to reduce our commitments and the number of things they have to engage with. I've got a couple of key leaders who I think are close to burning out actually.
Building confidence in others **Thinking about vulnerability in the whole organization**	**Sofia:** That's something we have to take really seriously—it's great that you are listening to the message behind what they are saying. Are you saying it's not that they are resisting change but it's that they feel they don't have the capacity to start something new and that's making them feel a little vulnerable? That's a bit of a different message from what you said in your letter, though.
	Mark: Yeah, true. It's hard to write that kind of thing down, though, especially to someone in your position. I feel a bit like the meat in the sandwich here.
Building a culture of support for change and reducing uncertainty	**Sofia:** That's not a great position to be in. We can change that. The district could support you with your reducing-commitments strategy. Would this help you? And the teachers? Or is there something else we can do? Then we can work out how to approach the inquiry material. We need to consider if the teachers are feeling vulnerable about inquiry and worry they don't know enough.

Developing Self-Regulation

What It Is

▶ Self-regulation is closely connected with metacognition, agency, and an evaluative mindset and underpins the capability to make and sustain change.

▶ Grow others' capacity to monitor, reflect, and make adjustments to their cognition and emotional responses and their ability to act strategically.

▶ Work across the multiple layers of a school to develop self-regulation to increase learning and positive change.

▶ Attend to emotion and motivation as part of self-regulation to enhance the chances of new practice becoming embedded.

Why It Matters

▶ Those who are responding to student learning needs (leaders and teachers) are empowered.

▶ Self-regulation is the engine that will continue to drive evaluative mindsets in the absence of outside help.

▶ Inquiry models are based on self-regulation of learning.

▶ Developing self-regulation in others shares power and underpins reciprocal relationships.

▶ The development of self-regulation is a critical part of formative assessment practice with students, so all layers of the school need to be self-regulating.

How I Do It

▶ Understand self-regulatory processes and be able to articulate to others how to do this.

▶ Model curiosity and metacognition about own learning through think-alouds.

▶ Scaffold others by providing support that fades as others take over tasks.

▶ Alongside handing over tasks, model and promote curiosity about the impact of the task, an evaluative mindset about outcomes from the task, and the ability to identify what is making a difference.

▶ Help others become aware of what they can do, develop their skills and knowledge, and help them see what they are responsible for.

Key Challenges for Me

▶ Knowing how to monitor own and others' learning in complex situations

▶ Managing own and others' motivations to self-regulate when things get hard

▶ Being explicit about your own self-regulation and bringing that language into conversation with adult learners

▶ Knowing when, what, and how to hand over processes and tasks

What I Should Notice

▶ How do others describe "what the problems are"? Do all participants see that it is "everyone *and* me"?

▶ Is the language of self-regulation becoming part of how leaders are thinking and talking about change and the issues?

▶ Am I scaffolding leadership that promotes self-regulation or inadvertently creating dependency?

online resources ↖

Available for download at https://resources.corwin.com/LeadingPowerfulPL

Developing Self–Regulation

What: Description of the Concept

> "Students [all learners] are more persistent in learning when they can manage their resources and deal with obstacles efficiently."
>
> (Boekaerts, 2010, p. 103)

Self-regulation can be thought of as part of the engine that continues to drive change once the PL program has ended. It is therefore a critical component of facilitating PL that promotes adaptive expertise. It is also a powerful concept at all levels of the system—significant for student learning, for teacher learning and practice, and for leadership of improvement.

Self-regulation is the process by which people monitor and reflect on their learning and behavior and make adjustments in response to evidence for increasing effectiveness (Zimmerman, 2002). It involves "self-generated thoughts, feelings, and behaviors that are oriented to attaining goals" (Zimmerman, 2002, p. 65) and involves having an evaluative mindset. Self-regulation is closely connected with metacognition (Root 5) or "thinking about our thinking," which is a cognitively focused process of monitoring one's thoughts and ideas.

Self-regulation includes emotional and social aspects too, recognizing the impact of emotion on learning. Boekaerts (2010) describes how regulating emotions in learning is as important as regulating cognitive processes and knowledge acquisition. Emotions and motivation are gatekeepers of learning (Dumont et al., 2010). This impacts on outcomes for all learners, students, and educators alike.

Another aspect of self-regulation is strategic action or agency, where learners act in accordance with their goals and reflections. Self-regulated learners will drive their learning by examining their thoughts and feelings about what and how they are learning and by seeking further knowledge as they identify gaps or areas of curiosity (Zimmerman, 2002).

What: Description of the Deliberate Act of Facilitation

Developing self-regulation as a DAF occurs when we take action that builds the leaders and teachers with whom we are working into self-regulated learners. Rather than stepping in or helping out, we choose to act in a way that encourages the leaders and teachers to monitor their own learning, be evaluative, examine and share their knowledge, develop their curiosity, and take strategic action. Developing self-regulation with educators across multiple layers of the school or context increases learning and supports positive and sustainable change. Educators need to be able to model self-regulation in order to develop self-regulation in others, especially their students.

> "My job is to keep power and responsibility in the schools. To do that I intentionally develop knowledge, skills and an evaluative mindset in leaders and teachers."
>
> (Facilitator)

Emotion is inextricably linked to our thinking and actions; therefore, learning to self-regulate emotion is a necessary aspect of self-regulation. When we become aware of triggers of our emotions, we can take positive action rather than react negatively. As educators we must be attuned to the impact of our emotion on others and on ourselves.

Why It Matters

Some of the strongest evidence for promoting deep learning and learning that can be transferred points to metacognition and self-regulation as fundamental (Bransford et al., 2000; Dumont et al., 2010; Pellegrino & Hilton, 2012). Developing self-regulation leads to deeper and more lasting learning as well as the urge to continue to learn, a necessary requisite for sustained and ongoing learning. This enables power and control to remain with the school, ultimately creating self-improving schools.

Self-regulation is at the heart of curricula, such as formative assessment practices, that value the competencies of their learners. It is therefore essential that leaders and teachers self-regulate, are able to articulate what it is, and know how to develop self-regulation in their learners, whether students or fellow members of the school.

Inquiry models of teacher PL (Timperley et al., 2014) are based on people, and then teams, becoming self-regulated learners—that is, learners who pose questions, gather information, and then check their progress and ask "What have I learned here?" and "What else do I need to know?" When teachers and leaders become self-regulated learners, they are able to recognize what they can and cannot do and what they need to do next. They become agents of change focused on improving learning rather than change followers who are dependent on external providers. Considering the change process as a joint responsibility positions us as coinvestigators, sharing power and forming reciprocal relationships.

How I Do It

There are three key approaches to promoting self-regulation with leaders and teachers: (1) developing your own self-regulation, (2) explicitly modeling self-regulation and metacognition through *talking aloud* about your thinking and feelings, and (3) scaffolding leaders and teachers to increase their self-regulation.

By being overtly self-regulated learners ourselves we can encourage others to learn in the same way. Modeling curiosity and thinking aloud when working through problems shows others what self-regulation and metacognition look and sound like. Deliberately sharing our feelings of vulnerability and uncertainty and how we self-regulate these feelings models how we approach and regulate new learning. Talking about our vulnerability helps to build trust and reduce perceived risks in failure.

> "It may become necessary for self-regulating learners to adjust or even abandon initial goals, to manage motivation and to adapt and occasionally invent tactics for making progress."
>
> (Butler & Winne, 1995, p. 245)

As well as scaffolding leaders and teachers into new tasks, also scaffold them into modeling and being explicit about self-regulation. A key to success in this work is to build leaders' and teachers' knowledge and skill and to be explicit with them about their abilities. As confidence and competence grow, so will a sense of curiosity and a desire to know more.

Critical actions for facilitators are recognizing what leaders and teachers know and can do, being curious about their perspectives, and acting to empower them rather than creating dependency. An orientation toward reciprocity rather than deficit thinking about leaders and teachers is a fundamental part of LCR practice. Reciprocity of this sort allows everyone's knowledge to be valued and builds self-regulation because people are recognizing what they know and what they need to know and seeking to learn that from others.

Language plays an important role in developing self-regulation as new terms and ideas can be tools for new thinking. This may require reframing and clarifying existing language that could otherwise get in the way. Changes in how things are described or words that are used can be important indicators of shifts in thinking. Right from the beginning, viewing ourselves as coinvestigators rather than experts helps share power, build respectful and reciprocal relationships, and develop joint responsibility for the change. Getting to know where leaders and teachers are through respectful questioning, reflecting back, and listening carefully can help provide a firm basis for building self-regulation.

Key Challenges for Me

Developing self-regulation in others demands a lot from facilitators who need to be aware of their own self-regulatory actions and strategies in order to be able to make them explicit to others. It can seem artificial or too deliberate to think aloud with others, but being explicit about our thoughts and feelings on issues or evidence can help those we are working with to learn how to do the same. When schools are beginning difficult PL journeys, looking inward and assessing their capabilities may be painful or risky for them. It can seem easier for them to hand responsibility for assessing and monitoring progress to others outside the school. However, it is important to keep ownership with the school team by developing their self-regulation as learners. Knowing when, what, and how to fade out support to avoid dependency is key. Self-regulation processes are invisible, and making them explicit requires the building of trust and sometimes courage to say that you don't know but want to find out.

It can also be a challenge for facilitators to self-regulate their learning as they take on new roles and responsibilities or begin to work in unfamiliar contexts. It can be hard to self-regulate our emotions at these times, and when things get hard, you are met with resistance or lack of motivation. Being able to monitor and reflect at these times can not only help us to make adjustments but also provide insight into authentic reflection and self-regulatory strategies that can be shared with others.

What I Should Notice

> "Sometimes I notice leaders seem reluctant to take on roles they need to, and I see it as my job to help them think aloud about what is getting in the way and how they might change their thinking."
>
> **(Facilitator)**

As self-regulation develops in leaders and teachers, we might see changes to roles, changes in orientation to PL, changes in language, and changes in relationships. Changes to roles might occur if people reorganize their ways of working when they become more self-regulating. If a team is operating as self-regulated learners they will all be taking responsibility for their own learning and will be able to reflect, contribute, and pose questions from an open-minded position of curiosity. This could manifest in new ways of working, new relationships among teams, and increased enthusiasm for and commitment to PL.

Language is important. Look for use of metacognitive language, overt reflection on learning and thinking, people beginning to use key words and phrases about monitoring their own learning, and more frequent posing of questions. It is also useful to regularly reflect on our own behavior and emotion. Am I continuing to self-regulate my new learning? Am I deliberately building self-regulation in others through think-alouds and self-regulatory language with a plan to fade out support or is dependency creeping back in?

Further Reading

Butler, D., Schnellert, B., & Perry, N. (2016). *Developing self-regulated learners.* Toronto, Canada: Pearson.

Pellegrino, J., & Hilton, M. (Eds.). (2012). *Education for life and work: Developing transferable knowledge and skills in the 21st century.* Washington, DC: National Academies Press.

Vignette 10a: Developing Self-Regulation

 Liam is working with a team of teachers in an elementary school who are conducting a joint inquiry into their teaching of writing to first and second graders. They are talking about the most recent set of reading results they have collated. Liam has been helping out by taking the results and making graphs, so the teachers can see who is progressing and at what rate. He makes graphs that show each student's trajectory, but he also makes some that show the progress of students who started at the same level and the progress of students from different backgrounds, so the teachers can see if some groups of students progress at a faster rate than others. Liam thinks that a way to grow teacher's capacity to self-regulate their learning would be to share this task with the teachers so that they can monitor the students' progress for themselves.

(Continued)

(Continued)

	Liam: So, here's the graph showing each student's progress, like we had last time.
	Zoe: These are great, you know, they just show it so clearly. Wow, some of these kids have really taken off. Look at that line!
	Margie: They are really valuable. Thanks, Liam! We've been sharing them with the principal too.
Modeling self-regulation through think-alouds	*Liam:* I'm glad they are useful. I guess the key thing isn't so much the graph itself but the decisions you make based on them, but the graphs do help to give a clear picture. When I looked at this, I noticed what Zoe mentioned how steep some of those lines are, and I wondered about who those students were and what you might have done to cause that acceleration.
	Margie: I wonder if it's the students who worked with the reading specialist for the extra sessions, although I think maybe they are starting a bit high for that. Maybe because those students were with the specialist, we were able to give more time to these ones.
	Zoe: Do you have the other graphs: the ones with the start points and groups on?
Growing capacity to monitor, reflect, and adjust	*Liam:* I thought we might make them together today, so you can see how it is done. It does help with the reflection process when you make them because you see the patterns emerging.
	Margie: I'm not sure we have the time or skills to do that.
Fading out support to grow self-regulation capacity	*Liam:* Well, let's give it a try, and we can talk at the end about what we'll do next time.

Vignette 10b: Developing Self-Regulation

 Fran is checking in with a high school leadership team. During this meeting she notices that one of the department chairs, usually a great contributor, is silent and fiddling with her pen. She seems upset and distracted. Fran decides to have a quiet word with her after the meeting.

Attending to emotion in self-regulation	*Fran:* You don't seem to be your usual self today, Eleanor. I hope everything is all right.
	Eleanor: Yeah, I'm okay. I'm just a bit over some of this, to be honest.
	Fran: Yeah? Over it?
	Eleanor: We're all doing our best, but all we get from the principal is more, more, more. I'm never going to get it right. Whatever I do is never going to be enough.
	Fran: You're feeling ground down by it all?
	Eleanor: Mmm-hmm. And everyone else is just saying "Yay, we're great, look at us," but half of it is not even true. They're just saying it.
Attending to emotion in self-regulation	*Fran:* That's frustrating. And tough for you if they're not being totally honest.
	Eleanor: There's just some people in my department, you know. They are not going to get on board with this, or anything else. Whatever I do it's "nope, not doing that, done it before, doesn't work." How am I ever going to get past that? It's like a brick wall.
	Fran: It is hard leading change, really hard. People resist in all kinds of ways.

	Eleanor: I guess I've just become too immersed in the negatives. I believe in the goals but not in my ability to bring them about.
Attending to emotion in self-regulation **Growing capacity to monitor, reflect, and make adjustments**	**Fran:** What's great is that you are starting to recognize what is happening and thinking about it. It's okay to have emotions about this stuff. It's tough, especially being the department chair and feeling responsible for your team. It's tough trying to deal with it on your own. I wonder who might be a good buddy or mentor for you in this work. A safe person for venting to and running things by.
	Eleanor: Well, there's Carmel. She's pretty down to earth and real.
	Fran: I'm happy to help you approach her on this if you like. She's chair of science, isn't she?

Providing Appropriate Support and Challenge

DAF
#11

What It Is

▶ Balance the need to challenge beliefs and routines while supporting others to change.

▶ Interrupt others' current theories of action and previously accepted routines and beliefs.

▶ Deepen understanding through challenge.

▶ Challenge existing assumptions and beliefs through the building of knowledge.

▶ Using appropriate challenge is difficult. It is determined by the context, the relationships and the problem to be discussed.

Why It Matters

▶ Change is unlikely or superficial if we do not challenge or interrupt existing beliefs that are problematic.

▶ Challenge without support can lead to nonengagement in change.

▶ Theories are often unconscious and difficult to change alone.

▶ Others can see things we don't.

▶ Support can increase the level of risk taken.

▶ Existing beliefs can be problematic for developing LCR practices.

How I Do It

▶ Challenge in ways that maintain respect.

▶ Build knowledge that challenges deeply held beliefs.

▶ Challenge using evidence.

▶ Revisit problematic beliefs—not necessarily in the moment.

▶ Keep in touch with how own actions are received.

▶ Prepare to challenge own beliefs, especially tacit ones.

▶ Deliberately consider what to support and what to challenge for each person.

Key Challenges for Me

▶ Balancing challenge and support—too much or little of either can lead to limited improvement

▶ Building of trust takes time

▶ Being surprised by unexpected responses

▶ Being careful about how we challenge others

▶ Challenging being particularly difficult at the start when relationships are new

What I Should Notice

▶ What beliefs and routines appear barriers to change?

▶ Could emotional responses suggest too much challenge?

▶ What support are individuals responding well to?

▶ What might you see if the support or challenge balance is working?

Providing Appropriate Support and Challenge

What: Description of the Concept

The concepts of support and challenge, when considered together, reveal that effecting change for improvement is a balancing act between providing support to learn something new while providing sufficient challenge to disturb or interrupt existing thinking in a way that initiates growth and change (Berry, 2008). Change is unlikely unless one's personal theories of practice are challenged. By providing both support and challenge, we recognize that both comfort and discomfort are a part of learning; we need to feel safe to learn, yet learning something new or unfamiliar can create discomfort, uncertainty, and perceptions of risk: "Opportunities to learn must occur in environments characterized by both trust and challenge because change is as much about the emotions as it is about knowledge and skills" (Timperley, 2008, pp. 15–16). Cognition and emotion are inseparable, and teacher emotions cannot be ignored in teacher change (Hargreaves, 1998).

> *"All learning activities require the twin elements of trust and challenge. Little professional learning takes place without challenge. Change, however, involves risk; before teachers take on that risk, they need to trust that their honest efforts will be supported, not belittled."*
>
> (Timperley, 2008, p. 16)

Providing support can include many different approaches, including encouraging change through building new knowledge and providing or ensuring a context of psychological safety (Edmondson, 1999). The provision of appropriate support creates a context in which individuals trust each other and are confident to take risks, believing that others will act in positive ways (Forsyth, Adams, & Hoy, 2011) and one where teachers are actively supported, encouraged ,and empowered through caring. Support is also referred to as safety or trust and may take particular forms such as scaffolding.

Providing challenge, on the other hand, sometimes involves creating feelings of discomfort for the learner. The learners' existing knowledge, beliefs, assumptions, and current practices are identified and interrupted, and they maybe have to reconsider and reconceptualize problematic worldviews. Sometimes these views may have been articulated, and other times the learner may not have been aware of them; both situations can feel very confronting. Challenge does not have to be direct: it can be indirect via the building of new knowledge (such as how to use first languages in classrooms) or exposure to different viewpoints when collaborating with others we do not usually work with. These different forms of new knowledge can challenge existing assumptions, leading to changes in teacher practices or the deepening and growth of existing understanding. Challenge has also been referred to as probing and nudging.

While being supported is usually a welcome experience, being challenged is usually an uncomfortable one because it involves a threat to our self-concept. If the discomfort is sufficiently strong, the learner may perceive a threat or risk to their professional and personal identities and respond with negative emotion or feelings of vulnerability, resulting in a reduction in engagement that limits rather than promotes learning (Twyford, 2016).

What: Description of the Deliberate Act of Facilitation

Providing support and challenge involves the deliberate use of challenge to initiate new learning while at the same time providing support to the learner. Doing this effectively for productive change is a lot about balance. Reaching or maintaining a balance of support and challenge is difficult, and unless we deliberately focus on the balance, we are likely to notice it only when it becomes out of balance and more difficult to restore. It is the difference between a constructive and an uncomfortable learning experience (Berry, 2008).

The individual, the context, the relationships, and the learning task or problem determine the degree of challenge and support needed for learning. Support and challenge should be tailored to the needs of the individual. Additionally, the stage in the learning process can impact on the balance. Timperley (2008) suggests there is a cyclical process of learning that begins with challenge to one's existing assumptions followed by a need to support new learning.

Similarly, Poekert (2011) reports that teachers needed "a good deal of pushing" after the introductory stage of support to ensure "greater possibilities for new learning" (p. 27). He concluded that a balance of scaffolding and nudging are needed to maximize learning.

Imbalance can occur when either the task or the relationships are privileged at the expense of the other, such as when challenge is avoided because of a focus on maintaining relationships or, by contrast, when the challenge belittles the learner. Imbalance can also happen when the gap between the known and the new learning is too great so that "the challenge becomes a threat and learning is inhibited" (Korthagen, 2001, p. 75).

> *"Expertise external to the group of participating teachers is necessary to challenge existing assumptions and develop the kinds of new knowledge and skills associated with positive outcomes for students."*
>
> (Timperley, 2008, p. 20)

Why It Matters

Providing appropriate levels of support and challenge matters because, when enacted in a balanced way, change and the development of new practices is more likely. It is known that change is unlikely or merely superficial if our beliefs are not engaged and that strongly held beliefs are difficult to change (Bransford et al., 2000). True conceptual change requires a level of discomfort and challenge, and this can be met with appropriate support.

Challenging problematic discourses has been identified as one of the key elements for PL linked to the promotion of positive and sustained student outcomes (Timperley et al., 2007). Problematic discourses that need to be challenged often relate to teachers' social constructions of students and their learning and how to teach particular curricula effectively. However, providing appropriate challenge to change others' beliefs and actions is not easy work, and leaders and facilitators have an important role. This role includes encouraging others to check their assumptions with evidence.

> "It's being brave, I think, and then also knowing that if you don't challenge the beliefs, the practice won't change. And it's also knowing that challenging beliefs isn't like a Taiaha (Māori weapon) thrown in their face—it's just probing the beliefs."
>
> (Facilitator)

Additionally, when leaders engage in constructive problem talk to discover why teachers and leaders do what they do—and the implications of these practices and alternate ones—they are more likely to help teachers change than if they avoid raising issues or blame others. The use of critique and debate of our ideas and practice as well as exposure to alternatives is important as a means of deepening understanding.

It is important to continually and deliberately consider how to provide a balance of support and challenge, and to remember it can be difficult to get it right. The norms of "non-interference, privacy and harmony" (Little, Gearhart, Curry, & Kafka, 2003) and notions of politeness (Wajnryb, 1996) often discourage people from challenging others' ideas and practices even though this is an important part of effective facilitation work.

How I Do It

The combined use of support and challenge should be deliberately considered for each learner on each occasion in recognition of the dynamic nature of relationships and the interdependent nature of emotion and cognition. The balanced combination of support and challenge is central to adaptive expertise and contributes to learning and change for improvement.

Maintaining respect and building trust while providing support and challenge is complex work and requires skillful application. There are suggestions in the literature to guide how to do this. Little and colleagues (2003) found evidence of facilitators who were able to challenge ideas and practices yet remain respectful and not crush the person. These facilitators provided consistent support such as meeting between events and demonstrating concern for the other person and their relationship. Stoll, Fink, and Earl (2003) list a range of support and challenge actions:

> Help others to self-evaluate; present examples from elsewhere in such a way that teachers can reflect on the relative merits of each; challenge people to broaden and extend their self-perception; "referee" discussions; encourage, praise, clarify and revisit issues to help people maintain momentum; and, where necessary, play the role of "confidant(e)." (p. 182)

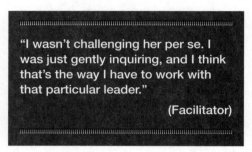

"I wasn't challenging her per se. I was just gently inquiring, and I think that's the way I have to work with that particular leader."

(Facilitator)

The use of clear evidence and knowledge building that questions the validity of the problematic belief or theory not only challenges but also provides an alternative explanation as a replacement.

Probing is one way that the idea of challenging can be enacted by facilitators (Colton, Langer, & Goff, 2015). When facilitators probe ideas, it can encourage teachers to delve into their thinking while building trust and respect. For example, as a facilitator you can probe for clarity that demonstrates your interest. Empowering probes presuppose the teacher's ability to understand and figure out solutions. It can also be important to probe for beliefs and feelings that encourage teachers to evaluate their thinking. At times "probes that cause cognitive dissonance or 'rattle one's brain'" (Colton et al., 2015, p. 44) may be important to use, with a warning that this may push some people beyond their comfort zone. This is why it is important to provide a balance of challenge and support. Protocols and clear guidelines for challenging others can provide a way of building challenge into facilitation work in a way that feels supportive.

Often as a facilitator you are expected to make in-the-moment decisions about when to challenge what has been stated or not stated in order to move the conversation along. However, revisiting problematic beliefs is also an accepted strategy, especially in new and/or difficult contexts, when you are not confident in that moment or when the beliefs to be challenged are deeply held and risky to challenge, such as race-based deficit theories.

As with all of the deliberate acts, we can reflect on our deliberate use of support and challenge and, perhaps more importantly, what gets in the way of us challenging others. Is it about needing courage or confidence in our ability to challenge? Being able to challenge and be challenged takes time and confidence to develop.

Key Challenges for Me

The key challenge to providing support and challenge is getting the balance right. Too much support creates dependent learners, while too much challenge can lead to nonengagement and damaged relationships, especially if that relationship was already fragile. Both scenarios jeopardize opportunities for educational improvement.

Another key challenge involves the unpredictability of people's responses to being challenged and reminds us of the complex number of variables to consider in facilitation work. Additionally the balance can change quickly and surprise us.

What I Should Notice

Listen for evidence of underlying beliefs and routines that could explain a lack of change or apparent inaction in teacher practice or a problematic interpretation of knowledge. If evident, then some form of challenge becomes unavoidable. It is important to check on the impact of your use of support and challenge with others. Negative emotional responses may be the result of too much challenge leading to increases in perceived risk and feelings of vulnerability. On the other hand, while it is relatively easy to see when you have used too much challenge, responses to support may go unnoticed and may need deliberate checking of their effectiveness for supporting change.

Additionally, it is not always easy to see when leaders and teachers want or are willing to accept support. Twyford (2016) says that teachers were less likely to ask for support from "experts" when they most needed it, preferring to ask trusted others. This suggests that deliberately providing support, rather than waiting to be asked, is important.

Further Reading

Colton, A. B., Langer, G. M., & Goff, L. S. (2015). Create a safe space to learn. *Journal of Staff Development, 36,* 40–45, 66.

Timperley, H. (2008). Teacher professional learning and development. *Educational Practices Series-18.* Geneva, Switzerland: International Academy of Education & International Bureau of Education.

Vignette 11a: Providing Appropriate Support and Challenge

S Sofia is working with a principal from one of the larger elementary schools in her district. They are talking about using inquiry for PL in the school. The math faculty is asking for funding to bring in an expert in mathematics education to share a new program for teaching problem solving. Sofia is eager to move toward using inquiry to work on student learning issues, with PL support provided when a need has been identified rather than paying for outside expertise that isn't targeted to learners and their needs. She thinks the request to fund the expert might arise from a belief about PL that isn't helpful to the school's progress.

	Sofia: Tell me about this math program and what you want to do.
	Brenda: Well, we heard a lot of good things about it at the state math association conference, and we had a chance to look at the materials. It's a problem-solving program to help us align to the Common Core, and they provide a facilitator to help you get started. They do four staff meetings, and you can buy extra sessions for smaller groups of teachers—which I think we'll need as we're a big school.
Challenge beliefs	*Sofia:* Uh-huh. Tell me about why you think this will make a difference? What will change as a result of doing this?
	Brenda: We need to modernize a bit, make our math programs more problem-solving based, so this will give us an easy way to do that. The program is really engaging. It includes technology stuff, student books, everything.
Interrupting theories of action	*Sofia:* So, I'm going to challenge you a bit here, try and tease this out. What is your theory in action here? What do you think this will do in terms of teacher learning—and change for students? Let's try and draw a diagram of what you are thinking. What's the basic need you are starting from? Modernization?
	Brenda: Common Core, I guess, the need to do problem solving, which we don't do much of at the moment.
Challenging beliefs and providing support	*Sofia:* Okay, so let's put that at the beginning with an arrow to the program. We have a curriculum need, so we move to this program. Now what? What will the program do?
	Brenda: I guess I'm jumping from introducing the program to it being implemented. If it was implemented, then our problem would be fixed, but now that we are talking about it I can see that there are a few "ifs" in there.
	Sofia: And my thinking is that those ifs are quite important. Could the ifs make this program less effective than you think?
	Brenda: Maybe. But I'm not sure what the alternative looks like. The teachers deserve something to help them.

Challenging through deepening knowledge	**Sofia:** That's true, and I'm not saying they won't get something. My idea though would be that we start with your learners and what they need. Then we ask this question: What do the teachers need to learn in order to meet our students' needs? That starts us off in a different way. I can get you some help with doing that process.
	Brenda: We would need support. It's a new way of thinking, but I can see that it would make the PL more useful, more connected to our real problems.

Vignette 11b: Providing Appropriate Support and Challenge

 Liam is working with the leader of a team of Grade 2 teachers who are looking at writing. He is sharing his semester overview with Liam. Each week they have a focus task that the children write about. Teachers then correct the work and type it out on the computer for the children to illustrate on Friday. Liam knows that the children are not making much progress in writing and is concerned that the teachers have a lot of control over the writing process: They chose the topic, the genre, do all the editing and proofreading, and present the children's work for them. He wants to explore the team's thinking around this and challenge some of their assumptions.

	Brad: This is the semester overview.
	Liam: Uh-huh. Tell me about how it's organized.
	Brad: Well, we have a really efficient system. It gets everyone working. Each week there's a focus, and then the children write after motivation. There's a few days for drafting, and then we correct their work and type it out. Friday is illustration day. We've been working off this overview for a couple of years now. It works well.
Interrupting theories of action	**Liam:** So, when we looked at the student data, we saw that there were some areas that the children weren't making much progress with . . . how does that feed in to the plan?
	Brad: The plan is there as a structure. It gives us the opportunity to help the children move on.
Challenging beliefs	**Liam:** I'd like to get into this a bit. It seems to me that some of the important tasks of writing, like editing or proofreading, are being done by teachers rather than students.
	Brad: They're too young for that really, and it takes them a long time and they don't get very far.
Challenging beliefs	**Liam:** I don't agree that they are too young. I think they could do it—and it might help them to develop their skills more quickly if they were engaged with all of the process.
	Brad: I'd need to see some evidence of what that looks like I think. I see our learners as pretty vulnerable, and if we don't help them along, they might just give up.
Providing support **Challenging through deepening knowledge**	**Liam:** I see them as capable. I suppose that might be where our theories differ. I have some videos I made with another school, showing their second-grade classes in action, which might be a place to start.

Co-Constructing Learning

DAF
#12

What It Is

⬤ Invite understanding of one another, and seek consensus around "what is going on here."

⬤ Deepen knowledge, shared meanings, and collaborative problem solving.

⬤ Embrace learning as a social process.

⬤ Enable power sharing within a safe environment where participants feel confident to share ideas.

⬤ Value all participants' contributions for shared knowledge building.

⬤ Promote and build reciprocal relationships of mutual respect to improve co-construction.

Why It Matters

⬤ The meaning of evidence, interactions, and language are always contextual.

⬤ Clarity of purpose and communication across the system are improved by learning from and with one another.

⬤ New understandings for change can develop via co-constructed collaborations.

⬤ Engagement and commitment to action are enhanced by co-constructing learning.

⬤ Relationships are strengthened through co-construction.

How I Do It

⬤ Build shared language and meanings.

⬤ Check for understanding and agreement.

⬤ Listen, notice, and monitor one's own impact.

⬤ Deliberately build community and trust through the process of co-construction.

⬤ Use tools such as the inquiry spiral to co-construct shared understanding and discuss concepts at a deeper level.

⬤ Value others' perspectives and knowledge, including learners and their families.

⬤ Create opportunities for others, including those not usually heard, to contribute in meaningful ways.

Key Challenges for Me

⬤ Working through the tension between "being asked and wanting to tell" versus co-constructing

⬤ Dealing with agenda-setting dilemmas

⬤ Needing more time to reach solutions and actions

⬤ Living with the discomfort inherent in co-construction

⬤ Changing how strategies for problem solving and decision-making are undertaken

What I Should Notice

⬤ What knowledge is at the table? Does it include learning principles, literature, theories, and research findings?

⬤ Whose voices are heard, and whose are missing?

⬤ What opportunities are there for co-construction?

⬤ How do leaders co-construct (share power) with teachers and other stakeholders?

online resources

Available for download at https://resources.corwin.com/LeadingPowerfulPL

Copyright © 2020 by Corwin. All rights reserved. Reprinted from *Leading Powerful Professional Learning: Responding to Complexity With Adaptive Expertise* by Deidre Le Fevre, Helen Timperley, Kaye Twyford, and Fiona Ell. Thousand Oaks, CA: Corwin, www.corwin.com. Reproduction authorized for educational use by educators, local school sites, and/or non-commercial or non-profit entities that have purchased the book.

Co-Constructing Learning

What: Description of the Concept

Learning is a social process, and co-construction is a way of working where knowledge and learning is constructed with others rather than seen as a process of delivery or transference of information from one person to another. Co-constructing learning is central to adaptive expertise and involves people working together to create shared understandings about the educational challenges they are working to problem solve and the way these might best be addressed.

> "Co-construction is generally viewed as having two (or more) people collaboratively construct a solution, an understanding, a shared meaning of knowledge, which neither partner possesses."
>
> (Chi, 1996, p. 5)

Social and affective processes mediate the co-construction of learning (Baker, Andriessen, & Jarvela, 2013). The quality of the relationships of the people involved affects the process. It can be more difficult to openly share our thinking when the quality of the existing relationship is fraught or not yet present. It is also important to recognize that what is shared may be constrained by a desire to maintain relationships (Robinson, Le Fevre, & Sinnema, 2017). Concerns over relationships can divert attention from the ideas and the thinking, resulting in "quick consensus-seeking" (Asterhan, 2013, p. 266), where limited co-construction of knowledge and/or critique occurs. Equally, co-construction of new knowledge is unlikely to occur in contexts where competitive behaviors such as winning at all costs are employed.

Personal values and beliefs also affect co-construction, as it is important to be open-minded and willing to value all participants' views. Genuinely respectful relationships are those where we as facilitators value others' perspectives, recognizing that they have particular knowledge about learners and the school community, for example, that we do not have.

Collaboration is typically considered synonymous with co-construction, although it is possible to collaborate at the more basic levels of informing and engaging without the essence of valuing others' contributions and sharing power and control, consistent with a co-constructive process.

What: Description of the Deliberate Act of Facilitation

> "'Real agreement' is thought to require both co-constructed shared understanding and agreement on these meanings."
>
> (Damşa, Ludvigsen, & Andriessen, 2013)

Co-constructing meaning, understandings, and solutions are fundamental for effective facilitation. Schools, and their various departments, are typically characterized by teachers and leaders who bring a diversity of thinking and beliefs about the problems they face. The meaning of evidence, purpose, interactions, and even words can be individually and contextually defined. This makes it essential for us to check and deliberately co-construct shared meanings that are locally defined and agreed upon. Checking for understanding and agreement is essential to keeping everyone on the same page and is foundational to being willing to learn new ways of thinking. Damşa et al. (2013) suggest real agreement:

Presupposes joint understanding . . . First, to create shared understanding requires co-construction; this cannot be done through simple accumulation of the contributions of individuals because each contribution is presumed to build on previous ones. Second, agreement needs to be established on the proposed meanings and solutions, and individual contributions—the "bricks of knowledge"—must be mobile and open to changes and elaborations. (pp. 110–111)

Rae Si'ilata, one of our research team, led a research project on facilitating LCR using Samoan bilingual texts. Rae brought the Pasifika concept of Talanoa Ako to our facilitation work: *Tala* means talk, and *noa* means to be free from the restrictions of *tapu*, in effect genuine dialogue that is co-constructed and unrestricted. Her Pasifika lens required that we use a co-constructed approach to the PL, one that values the contributions of all to shared knowledge building. This reminds us that the context affects co-construction.

> "If you're aware of the person and you want to really get to know that person and know how and what they're thinking then that is more likely to make you more co-constructive with them rather than directive."
>
> (Facilitator)

Genuine, respectful relationships, promoted and built by facilitators, improve co-construction. People are more likely to participate and share their thinking if the environment is safe and encourages people to feel confident that they can share.

Why It Matters

Co-construction is an important way of working as a facilitator because meaning is socially and contextually mediated. Talking with one another is an essential first step in the development of shared meanings that are necessary to drive change. These shared meanings include the meaning of evidence, interpretations of interactions, and shared language. Shared language is essential for effective co-construction as it provides a vehicle or tool to progress the development of shared meaning and understanding of "what's going on here." The use of shared language improves communication throughout the system.

Research into how people learn tells us that new knowledge is built on existing knowledge and beliefs and that if this prior knowledge is ignored then new learning may be different to that intended (Bransford et al., 2000). By creating opportunities to communicate within and across the system, we are more likely to understand other peoples' current thinking, and this can be an important place from which to continue co-constructing new understandings with them. Co-construction has been linked to producing deep learning and removing misconceptions. Additionally, new understandings, connections, and innovative solutions become possible when multiple voices are heard. This is thought to occur through the cognitive dissonance that is created from hearing different perspectives from our own or ones we may not have considered.

Working co-constructively demands valuing and respecting others. Day-to-day interactions can build and strengthen relationships, which in turn increases engagement in co-construction. Engagement and commitment to act are enhanced through co-constructed conversations that build ownership and buy-in of the shared purpose.

How I Do It

Co-construction requires deliberate attention to building shared language and meanings. Tools such as the spiral of inquiry (Timperley et al., 2014) and conceptual frameworks such as the Va'a Tele model (Si'ilata) can be used to develop a shared language, co-construct shared understandings, and discuss concepts at deeper levels. They also provide a platform for discussing issues and processes that may otherwise be sensitive or likely to be taken personally.

> "I try and work so that they feel they have ownership in their own professional learning. It's not being done to them. It's being co-constructed with them and so therefore they feel safe to confront their own practices and beliefs and make changes . . . because it's actually about problem solving together."
>
> (Lead facilitator)

An integral aspect of co-constructing involves checking for understanding and agreement. This is essential to keeping everyone on the same page and can be the start of new learning. We can do this by listening carefully for participants' existing knowledge and connecting new knowledge to existing conceptual frameworks and practices that leaders and teachers already have.

Co-constructing involves continually checking and being aware of our impact on the process. This involves deliberately checking in to see if shared meanings have become established and whether agreement has been reached and by whom. At other times it is important to check how we are co-constructing or whether we have defaulted to telling.

Genuine co-construction depends on quality relationships, which in turn are strengthened through the processes of collaboration. As facilitators, we can deliberately co-construct with others to build the quality relationships that are essential for effective facilitation. We can develop trust and respect by valuing others' perspectives and the knowledge they bring to co-construction. This means paying attention to those voices that are not traditionally heard such as learners and their families. Facilitators can do this by creating opportunities for them to contribute to the improvement efforts in meaningful ways.

Key Challenges for Me

Learning from and with one another is not without tensions and challenges. While creating opportunities for people to work together is an important deliberate act, it is insufficient to guarantee co-construction. In our research into LCR, facilitators and inquiry leaders reported tension between co-constructing learning and wanting to be provided with an agenda for learning in both their school-based and group sessions. This has been referred to as the agenda-setting dilemma in a constructivist or co-constructed PL context (Richardson, 1992). Richardson refers to the way facilitators can feel conflicted about their own agency, or the extent to which they want to influence the direction of learning, in contrast to co-constructing learning. Being able to live with the discomfort and degree of uncertainty around co-constructing PL may be a necessary aspect of LCR facilitation. The agenda-setting dilemma is confounded by the fact that we don't always know what we don't know or need to know.

Another challenge when choosing to co-construct meaning with others concerns time. On the surface it seems that telling takes much less time to reach a solution and take action. However, without the construction of new knowledge and shared understanding, the planned outcome may well be compromised as people bring their own interpretations to guide their actions.

Co-construction as a way of working requires a different mindset and routines for problem solving and decision-making from what typically happens in schools. Busy leaders and teachers may need persuading to see that the time required and discomfort inherent in working co-constructively with others, and with larger groups of people, will in due course lead to better outcomes.

What I Should Notice

In addition to listening for others' existing theories and beliefs, it is important to notice the legitimacy of the knowledge that is shared as well as the power relations that exist when leaders and teachers work collaboratively. This involves checking the knowledge for assumptions and misunderstandings based on learning principles and research.

Power relations refers to the patterns of interaction that occur, such as whose voice is the loudest and attracts the least critique or the most agreement, along with noticing the silent or missing voices at the table. In some situations, there may be leaders who work autocratically and do not provide opportunities for co-construction on important issues and instead focus on informing (telling) others what they are expected to do. Alternatively, leaders may invite co-construction yet dismiss the outcomes and expect their views to prevail.

Further Reading

Baker, M., Andriessen, J., & Jarvela, S. (Eds.). (2013). *Affective learning together: Social and emotional dimensions of collaborative learning.* Oxon, England: Routledge.

Damşa, C., Ludvigsen, S., & Andriessen, J. (2013). Knowledge co-construction—Epistemic consensus or relational assent? In M. Baker, J. Andriessen, & S. Jarvela (Eds.), *Affective learning together: Social and emotional dimensions of collaborative learning* (pp. 106–129). Oxon, England: Routledge.

Vignette 12a: Co-Constructing Learning

L Liam is having his second session with a team of Grade 3 teachers, looking at reading. Last time it became clear to Liam that the teachers seemed confused about the main issue and what a possible solution might be. There was also some confusion about Liam's role: the teachers thought he was there to provide them with some input, to tell them about new resources or techniques. Liam thought he was there to help them frame an inquiry into what was happening in reading for their learners. There is quite a lot of pressure on Liam to tell the teachers what he thinks. They are positioning him as an expert and asking for the solution. He is finding it hard to lead the conversation and wants to avoid conflict—and he could just tell them. Liam knows, however, that although that is tempting, it's a short-term fix because whatever he tells them is unlikely to stick in practice, and the teachers need to have agency and buy-in to both the process and the conclusions.

Seeking consensus	**Liam:** So, last time we met we got in a bit of a muddle. I'd be interested to hear from you about where you think we got to.
	Tina: Well, we spent a lot of time looking at our data and talking about individual kids, but I'm not sure where we got to really. I think we were hoping for a bit more direction from you.
Sharing power **Using co-constructed conversation to problem solve**	**Liam:** Sure, I understand that, but I think we need to take our time and work together to define what we are focusing on and share ideas about what we could do. After all, I might know some things, but you are the experts on your students, and I know there's quite a lot of expertise in reading teaching just sitting here.
	Tracey: Okay, so I've been thinking about this since last time, and I think where we were going off course was with what we think reading is: whether we are talking about decoding the words or reading comprehension, or both, I think we were talking past each other a bit.
Inviting understandings	**Liam:** Hmm, thanks Tracey—thoughts from anyone else?
	Taylor: I can see what you mean I think, Tracey, I was focusing on reading comprehension, but even within that I think there are some different pieces we need to pick up on—different levels, or steps.
	Tina: Understanding meaning, linking to what they know, inferring from text . . .
Building shared meanings	**Liam:** Whoa, hang on. Let's record some of this so we can have something to refer back to together. So, everyone can give their ideas. I'll be the secretary on this whiteboard here. Tracey, you had the first distinction. What was that?
	Tracey: Reading as having different parts—I was thinking of decoding and then comprehending . . .

Vignette 12b: Co-Constructing Learning

 Mateo and his department are striking some problems teaching the Grade 7 students about ratios and proportional reasoning. The students have done poorly on a midpoint assessment, and the teachers are confused about why their plans aren't leading to better results. This year they have been piloting an online platform for some of their teaching, which they thought would improve the students' basic skills, but the opposite seems to be happening.

Inviting understanding and seeking consensus	*Mateo:* Well, here's an interesting problem for us. We seem to be going backward rather than forward with our new program. I'm a bit disheartened by this. What do you think is going on?
	Maria: The students seemed really motivated by working on the laptops. I was expecting big gains judging by the engagement levels.
Problem solving through co-constructed conversation	*Elisa:* There was a bit of time wasting though—but not really enough to account for this. I know the program is self-adjusting but maybe when they were sitting there, they were just getting them all wrong rather than actually learning the stuff.
	Maria: Yeah, maybe, I guess doing lots of practice of something wrong isn't going to help. Maybe we need to look more closely at the spreadsheet of what they are doing. It's just so detailed it's hard to see.
Valuing all contributions	*Mateo:* Thomas, what do you think?
	Thomas: Well, I was just looking at the program again and looking at the assessment, and there's not a lot of direct overlap. We used last year's assessment again, but we didn't really account for what the program focuses on. It's really more that the program presents the problems in a different way to the test—and we've assumed that the students would recognize the ideas in the new context.
	Maria: Which they should if they understood them . . .
Problem solving through co-constructed conversation	*Elisa:* Maybe what this means is that in past years they only did better than this because we taught using examples like the ones they'd get in the test, not because they really had a deep knowledge.
	Thomas: I don't think the program aims for deep knowledge, but we've been expecting transfer back without explicitly teaching it.
Deepening knowledge and shared meanings	*Mateo:* I wonder if we are clear about what we think deep knowledge of this material is. It's partly rote procedures, conversions, and stuff, but underneath that it's very powerful concepts—fundamental stuff about proportional reasoning.
	Elisa: Do we need to work up a bit of a diagram or something of what we think we are aiming for and then map the program activities onto it? See where the gaps are?

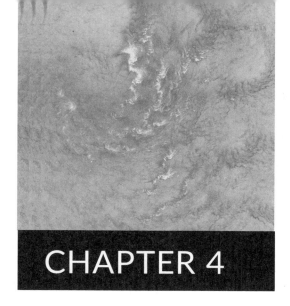

CHAPTER 4

Facilitating Improvement

Adaptive expertise, at its essence, is about responding to complex educational problems in ways that promote improvement and equity in education. This chapter is intended to bring together and guide facilitation work and help focus efforts in effective and rewarding ways. First, the chapter revisits the importance of adaptive expertise to enable educators and leaders be effective in their work and efficient with resources in facilitating ongoing and sustainable improvement within and across education systems. Next, adaptive expertise is situated in relation to other forms of expertise that are necessary to enable improvement in education. Key ideas regarding what it means to develop adaptive expertise are explored from both the perspective of developing one's own adaptive expertise as a facilitator, leader, or administrator and developing the adaptive expertise of others. The chapter finishes by highlighting some of the ideas that are intended to be kept front and center in the challenging and important work of facilitating improvement.

Facilitating Improvement and Adaptive Expertise

So the story goes . . . Albert Einstein was talking with his students and handing out exam papers when one of the students queried Einstein. The student had noticed that Einstein had set the same exam questions for the class as the previous year. "Yes!" replied Einstein, who quickly explained that the questions were indeed the same . . . but the answers would be different this year. We can't be sure whether or not this story is accurate; however, the idea is relevant to the work of facilitating improvement. It can feel like the same questions persist in education for years on end. Yes, indeed we have been grappling with many of the same questions in education for some time. Questions such as "How can we best serve our most vulnerable students?" "What makes the facilitation of professional learning (PL) effective?" and "How can we bring about sustainable change for improvement in education?" are longstanding. These same questions are likely to persist, but the ways we need to respond to them will change. This is why adaptive expertise is such a practical and powerful concept to use when thinking about how to facilitate improvement.

Effectively facilitating improvement in education demands keeping students at the center of all improvement efforts, particularly those students whose educational needs are not well served by current approaches to education. Many times, we may not be working directly with students—for example, we may be facilitating improvement through working with communities, families, leaders, professional colleagues, teachers, or policy makers—yet the central focus of facilitation for improvement needs always to be students. This involves responding to questions such as "What do the adults in this situation need to know, feel, and do to to be able to respond to the needs of students?" or the more challenging question "What are we currently doing or not doing that is creating inequitable outcomes?" This persistent focus on students is central to the concept of adaptive expertise presented in this book.

How can one learn to respond in ways that use adaptive expertise? This in itself is complex as learning needs to be both self-guided but also mediated by others. It can seem tempting to believe that educators can simply become "self-educated" because all that people need to learn is available at their fingertips through books and online resources. The risk, however, is that in doing this, people continually self-select and learn in ways that reinforce what they already believe, self-selecting information that confirms their existing theories and reinforcing existing practices. Instead, the sort of learning that is needed to develop adaptive expertise is deliberately informed by evidence and mediated by others. Learning that is deliberately informed by evidence is informed by robust evidence specific to a context of practice as well as by broader theories of learning and improvement. Learning that is mediated by others is learning that challenges you to reconsider existing beliefs, to try new ways of approaching problems, and to question the effectiveness of familiar ways of responding. To be able to respond in new and novel ways means we need to intentionally interrupt existing automatic ways of responding (Katz & Dack, 2013). Why is intentional interruption important in developing adaptive expertise? People tend to engage in the world in ways that confirm what they already know or believe, and it is difficult to get beyond this, particularly in roles that educators and leaders have where there are so many demands on them constantly that it can feel as if there is not even time to think.

Adaptive expertise has the potential to thrive in cultures of collaborative professionalism where there is intentional interruption (Hargreaves & O'Connor, 2018). What is meant by collaborative professionalism? In contrast to problem solving being seen as an individual task, and a top-down effort whereby those with most authority in an organization are the "experts," adaptive expertise can thrive within a culture that intentionally engages people together in learning and problem solving. This way of working together can promote collective agency or efficacy in terms of the responsibility being more widespread across educators as they work together within schools and across to develop effective responses to complex problems. When educators hold high expectations, are persistent in their intentional efforts, and collectively believe that their responses can make a difference, student achievement increases (Donohoo, 2017).

How Does Adaptive Expertise Fit With Other Forms of Expertise?

The analogy of driving a car can be helpful when thinking about adaptive expertise. Driving a car is something that becomes easier with experience and time. It requires less attention when the driver is experienced, the road is familiar, the weather is good, and the journey is not far. There are many tasks involved in driving that one learns to do almost automatically without conscious awareness once you are an experienced driver—thus, a driver employs much routine expertise. However, being a safe driver when the unexpected arises demands adaptive expertise. It requires being able to do many things almost automatically or routinely yet at the same time making continual judgments about the road conditions, your speed, other drivers around you, the state of the car, and how you should respond to drive safely.

To be a safe and effective driver demands both being able to respond automatically in ways that are predictable and familiar and also being able to respond in new and novel ways to unexpected and complex events, such as on a rural road when an animal runs out in front of the car. Importantly, it also involves being able to recognize the difference. This might happen almost subconsciously, but a safe and effective driver is continually moving in and out of responding automatically with routine expertise and employing adaptive expertise. It is possible to compare driving a car to facilitating PL for improvement. Some parts of the work of facilitation are more predictable than others, some contexts are more familiar than others, and some problems have more clearly defined solutions than others. Given the complexity of student needs it is important to be able to move in and out of using routine and adaptive expertise almost synchronistically depending on the complexity of the problem or situation and, therefore, the complexity of the response needed.

How do you recognize when a context presents a clearly defined problem with a clear solution demanding routine expertise, or when it is a complex context with no clearly defined solution demanding adaptive expertise?

A recurring mistake in education is thinking that problems are simple when in fact they are complex. Indeed, very few problems in educational settings will be simple, routine problems. It may seem easy to propose linear or causal relationships between things, such as teacher PL and student achievement, but experience and research suggest that such relationships are anything but linear or casual.

There are some telltale signs that a problem is complex and not simple. Interventions have been tried (maybe small-group teaching has been established), but results have been mixed and not what would have been expected for the effort expended. On the other hand, something small, an offhand comment or a newspaper column, causes unexpectedly large changes in practice. Sometimes a series of workshops and classroom observation result in no observable change in practice six months later. Despite people "talking the talk," there is little action or improvement. No one can really explain why the agreed-upon changes have not been implemented. These things all result from complexity: the outcomes of any action will be unpredictable, the effects of efforts may be out of proportion with their size, and it may feel like you are "missing the key" as you try to pull apart and analyze the problem.

If a problem can be understood by analyzing its parts, it is complicated not complex, and a simple, known solution may exist to remedy it. However, very few educational problems are like this. It is easier to think of examples such as the school security alarm being triggered by teachers coming in after hours. Working out what they are doing wrong by watching them set the alarm will probably result in finding a straightforward, known solution. Educational problems are usually characterized by complexity because they involve people and learning, which are two complex phenomena. Even seemingly simple routines, such as giving a spelling assessment or putting children in groups, can be seen as complex. The ways we assess and group can lead to unintended consequences for equity in our classrooms and intersect with students' linguistic and cultural backgrounds in complex ways.

Being an effective facilitator of improvement can become easier with time; however, time is not sufficient. To be an effective facilitator one must be able to do many things almost automatically while at the same time continually scanning the environment to check how people are responding, what they are understanding, and how relevant the focus of the work is to the particular problems of practice. In effective facilitation work, leaders and facilitators are always working from a base of adaptive expertise. What this looks like, however, will vary depending on the nature of the context and the problems they are trying to solve. Known and predictable situations enable more automatic or routine responses, so the level of responsiveness is not as high as that needed in uncertain and unpredictable contexts.

Figure 4 represents how different types of expertise interact in facilitation. As the complexity of a problem increases, the complexity of the response needed increases, demanding adaptive expertise. Adaptive expertise is essential for working with complex problems, and it is central to effectively facilitating PL that supports educators to address complex problems. Complex problems and the type of response required is represented in the upper right quadrant of Figure 4.

However, there is also a place for routine expertise—as can be seen in this figure. Routine expertise wherein educators and leaders draw on existing knowledge and ways of responding can be efficient for addressing clearly defined problems with known solutions. It is indeed an efficient way of responding in such contexts. Not all situations require adaptive expertise, and it would be a drain on people's already limited cognitive capacity and energies to suggest that they do. The lower left quadrant represents facilitation that is predominantly characterized as engaging routine expertise. It is labeled predominantly because often an element of adaptive expertise is needed.

The other two quadrants represent inefficient and ineffective responses. The top left quadrant is inefficient because complex responses are not so necessary for clearly defined problems; they are in some ways a waste of cognitive resources and time. On the other hand the lower right quadrant represents ineffective responses because complex problems demand complex responses.

The upper right quadrant represents the sorts of educational problems and contexts that have been the focus of this book. These are the complex, ongoing problems that are difficult to address. These are the problems that require adaptive expertise. In the past, education has tended to treat many of these complex problems in routine ways, and this has not been effective as current disparities in student outcomes demonstrate.

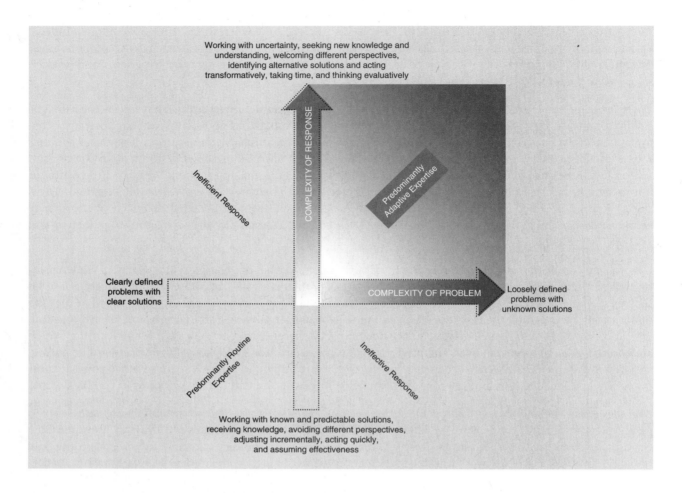

While clearly defined problems, sometimes referred to as "technical" problems, tend to be able to be addressed using familiar or routine expertise and existing knowledge, complex problems or "adaptive challenges" require learning, reconsidering existing ways of working and responding in new ways (Heifetz & Linsky, 2017). Ongoing learning is therefore central to adaptive expertise. Progress toward improvement requires changing ways of thinking, learning, and operating because the solutions to complex problems lie beyond current ways of operating.

Developing Your Own Adaptive Expertise

Throughout this book you have been encouraged to consider how to develop your own adaptive expertise, what to notice, and what some of the key challenges you encounter may be. It is important to keep in mind all components of the conceptual model represented in the tree diagram presented in the Introduction as these all interact to enable adaptive expertise.

The core components are shown in Figure 5. The roots of the tree represent the personal qualities and dispositions that are fundamental to adaptive expertise. With practice, support, and feedback, it is possible to develop these ways of thinking, feeling, and acting. Although all six roots are important and interact, in developing your own adaptive expertise you might try focusing on one at a time to really hone and develop each disposition. Which of the roots do you think are your strength already? Where is there room for development? What might others say about you if you asked them this question? These personal qualities and dispositions are not static but are ways of being that can be honed and developed over time.

The trunk represents the central focus of responsiveness, which is core to adaptive expertise. This responsiveness needs to be driven by the intention to improve valued educational outcomes for all students but, in particular,

those who are currently and historically least well served. The trunk represents a generative improvement orientation that focuses on generating energy toward achieving equity in outcomes for all learners. Questions you might ask yourself as you develop your own adaptive expertise include the following: Who are the learners that I most need to focus on? What are the key relationships that are important to nurture to enable me to do this work? How will I know if we are getting closer to achieving important and valued outcomes of equity for these learners?

The three branches—(1) purpose and focus, (2) knowledge and inquiry, and (3) effective learning processes—represent the deliberate acts of facilitation (DAFs), the decisions, and practices that are important to develop in your adaptive expertise. Developing your own capacity to engage effectively in these DAFs demands knowledge. For this reason, Further Reading suggestions are provided, and you will no doubt add your own valued resources to these as you work. However, it would be remiss to imply this is straightforward and easy to do. Developing adaptive expertise also requires learning to live with a degree of acceptance with "not knowing" and continually seeking to better understand. This can feel uncomfortable and unsettling. Developing your own adaptive expertise is a continual process of learning, questioning, and being willing to be vulnerable, just like the leaf "navigating perceptions of risk" in the tree. This can be easier to do when working in professional settings of mutual trust and respect.

Developing Adaptive Expertise in Others

Schools are often hierarchical organizations where people may default to waiting for someone in a more senior position to solve a problem. This type of dependency is not effective for solving problems using adaptive expertise. It is essential, therefore, to develop adaptive expertise in others so that all those in schools are empowered and knowledgeable. It is important to create supportive networks in which facilitators and leaders can talk about their work. Trust and respect are important conditions for developing expertise in others as this requires joint responsibility, collaboration, and support.

Developing expertise in others is essential in creating systemic improvement in education. It is not the intention to develop pockets of improvement in some schools or districts, but rather the goal has to be to promote widespread and lasting improvement across all schools and districts. Pockets of adaptive expertise will not enable such systemic improvement. You might use this book to guide others in the development of and focus on their own adaptive expertise.

Putting It All Together

In this chapter, adaptive expertise has been presented using the metaphor of a tree. The roots provide the foundation and the personal qualities and ways of being that are essential to underpin adaptive expertise. The trunk is grounded by the personal qualities represented in the roots and keeps the focus on outcomes for learners. The trunk represents being responsive in ways that promote improvement and represents the importance of relationships in achieving this. The branches and leaves represent the actual acts of facilitation that are central to developing adaptive expertise; indeed, they represent adaptive expertise in action. One of the things about a concept such as this is it is complex and can feel difficult to understand. The metaphor of the tree is intended to help educators comprehend the key parts that are essential to pay attention to.

Leading PL for powerful change is demanding work. "Most forms of adaptive failure are a product of our difficulty in containing prolonged periods of experimentation, and the difficult conversations that accompany them" (Heifetz, 2010, p. 76). Facilitators and leaders have an important role in understanding the emotional as well as the cognitive and practical challenges in working with uncertainty and responding effectively. Honoring the complexity and being willing to live with uncertainty and ongoing change can feel like tough work; however, it is important not to feel overwhelmed. The book has been intentionally designed to enable you to dip into sections and focus your attention on parts of the facilitation work since it is ineffective and inefficient to try to learn everything at once. As you continue in your facilitation and leadership work, ask yourself the following questions: What is hard for me here? What might I pay attention to in the model that could help me here? What shall I focus on next?

It is not uncommon to get to the end of book like this and look for a checklist: What do I have to do next? What do I need to remember? Tempting though it is to simplify these complex ideas and bring everything together into a simple to-do list, there is no checklist here as it would be contradictory to the very concept of adaptive expertise. Rather, it is the complexity of effective facilitation for promoting professional and student learning that needs to be kept alive: This is the challenge for educators and leaders. Rather than completing a checklist, perhaps you can write your own reflections: What is it I need to support me in doing this work? What will help me when others just want me to tell them what to do? This is difficult work, but you are not alone in this.

Perhaps one of the hardest things in responding to complexity with adaptive expertise is the need to be comfortable with not knowing, with not having a definitive direction of what to do next (Heifetz, 2010). Recognizing that we are working in a complex situation reassures us that it's all right to "not know," and adaptive expertise gives us a framework for responding effectively. By working together with others and using adaptive expertise, we can be in a strong position to serve our most vulnerable learners.

Research Appendix

The model of adaptive expertise in facilitation presented in this book, and the tree metaphor associated with it, emerged from a systematic program of research that was conducted alongside a large professional learning (PL) initiative over a five-year period. This research appendix first describes adaptive expertise, the theoretical basis of the program of research. A brief description of each of the studies on which the model is based follows the theoretical framework.

Adaptive Expertise: Where Does It Come From, and How Is It Different?

The idea of adaptive expertise was first proposed by Hatano and Inagaki (1986). They proposed a way of mapping levels of innovation against levels of efficiency. Practitioners who were highly efficient but did not innovate much were described as *routine experts*. Practitioners who innovated a lot but were not very efficient were described as *frustrated novices*. Practitioners who were highly innovative and also very efficient were described as *adaptive experts*. Adaptive experts were capable of responding to changed circumstances with efficiency and insight. Routine experts were experts but experts at performing learned routines rather than experts in reading situations and selecting appropriate responses. In particular they were not expert in responding in new or novel ways. This basic idea appealed to many people interested in teacher professionalism and teacher learning because it offered a way to characterize the in-the-moment thinking and decision-making that constitutes effective teaching.

The term *adaptive expert* suggests that a person can become an adaptive expert and remain so forever. In fact, adaptive expertise has a lot to do with the contexts in which it is practiced, as the act of being responsive of necessity includes the context one is responding to. For this reason, we moved from *adaptive expert* to *adaptive expertise*—adaptive expertise is displayed by people in their practice, in certain contexts, and in a range of ways. A person may have adaptive expertise in one context but not in another. The key concept to recognize is that adaptive expertise and routine expertise differ qualitatively from each other. They are different orientations and have different goals. Often in education we have looked to develop routine experts, those who can readily enact preset routines, such as a sequence of phonics tasks or a mathematics share out session. This tendency is reflected in the use of the word *training* to describe teacher preparation and the proliferation of skills-based teacher preparation and PL programs, where teachers learn to enact particular routines or protocols. Developing adaptive expertise involves a different mindset about what it means to learn and teach. Adaptive expertise requires preparation for sophisticated, evidence-based decision making, which requires a strong knowledge base and an open mind. It also requires questioning assumptions, understanding where our judgments come from, and paying attention to the way others see things. Using adaptive expertise does not mean routines are never performed. Routines are a necessary and important part of coping with demanding situations to avoid cognitive overload. Adaptive expertise, however, emphasizes the choice of a routine over performing it without reference to its impact or suitability in context.

The idea of adaptive expertise has appeal in particular because of the fast pace of change in the world and the uncertain future for which our students need to be prepared. Education needs to be flexible and responsive, as well as promote equity and transformation, if it is to contribute to the challenges that face our world. Routine expertise seems inadequate in the face of these challenges.

Adaptive expertise as a way of conceptualizing teacher professionalism has gained traction in recent years. What remains largely unconsidered is how to develop adaptive expertise, especially through leadership and PL. The research that led to this book was undertaken in order to find out what kinds of facilitation built adaptive expertise in others. If we want teachers to tackle classroom challenges using adaptive expertise, how can we help them to develop it? Bransford and colleagues (2010) explain that adaptive expertise can be a property of organizations and groups as well as a characteristic of individuals, so facilitators are sometimes trying to develop schools with adaptive expertise as well as help leaders and teachers to move toward these ways of working. We wanted to find out what facilitators, who developed adaptive expertise in others, believed, said, and did. Our findings formed the base of the suggestions and explanations in this book.

A Definition of Adaptive Expertise in Facilitation

As a first step to exploring adaptive expertise in facilitation we developed a definition based on the literature and previous research by members of our team. The definition has many parts, reflecting the complex nature of adaptive expertise. This book uses the metaphor of a tree to provide examples of adaptive expertise in action, describing them one by one in order to make these different parts of the definition explicit. A key element of the tree metaphor is that adaptive expertise involves a complex, integrated whole. The key elements of the definition are reflected throughout this book.

Adaptive expertise is a way of working in complex environments that focuses on learning and change for the purpose of improving valued outcomes. Adaptive expertise draws on deep conceptual knowledge and a well-honed skill set. It is a holistic approach, driven by inquiry, underpinned by curiosity, responsiveness, and willingness to learn and change. Adaptive expertise is highly metacognitive and involves self and co-regulated learning through continuous cycles of action and deliberate reflection. Individuals, organizations and larger systems can demonstrate adaptive expertise in the way they respond to evidence about outcomes and create new understandings and ways of working in their attempts to improve them for learners. Adaptive expertise involves seeking transformative and sustainable improvement at all levels of the system. Policy makers, leaders, teachers and young people all benefit from development of their adaptive expertise.

(Le Fevre, Timperley, & Ell, 2015)

The Studies

The research on which this book is based took place alongside a five-year nationwide PL initiative. There were three main strands to the work. One strand monitored the progress of students in the schools that engaged with the PL—to see if there were changes in student achievement in the focus areas of reading, writing, and mathematics. Schools sent beginning and end-of-year standardized data, with individual identifiers to allow for student matching, to a central database for all the years they were involved in the PL. A substantial database, which could be used to identify schools that were accelerating student achievement, was built from this information. This strand is not the focus of this book, but the collated evidence of change in student achievement was used to select facilitator participants for some of the studies. The second strand focused on adaptive expertise and PL. Each year's work built on the findings of the previous year, so over time we were able to build toward the model presented in this book. Research findings were fed back to the PL group twice a year, allowing for co-construction of knowledge and reciprocal sharing of information and ideas. This process meant that our research findings were always examined closely by those who would use them, and we were challenged to make them relevant and useful.

The third strand focused on understanding the nature and impact of perceptions of risk on educators after it became clear in the findings in the first year that uncertainty and perceived risk in change were part of teachers' and leaders' work but also for the facilitators, especially when working for improvement and social justice.

The next section summarizes four of the key studies that contributed to the model and tree metaphor presented in this book. This is followed by a summary of our research into educators' perceptions of risk.

Deliberate Acts of Facilitation

In this study a group of four facilitators worked with the research team to analyze their practice—in particular making explicit their decision making and actions during facilitation conversations. The facilitators were purposively selected and invited to take part based on their successful record of improvement in student achievement in the schools that they worked with. They came from different regions of New Zealand and worked in a wide range of schools from large, urban multicultural settings to smaller, rural, largely indigenous communities and isolated, remote schools in small communities. They typically had backgrounds as teachers and school leaders before becoming facilitators. This study included analysis of transcripts of leadership development conversations between facilitators and school leaders. The leadership development conversations were rich sources of information about the choices of the facilitators as they worked to build adaptive expertise in the school leaders.

The Research Questions

This study sought to answer the following questions:

- What do facilitators do in leadership development conversations with school leaders to deliberately build adaptive expertise?
- What considerations underpin their choices and decisions in leadership development conversations?

Data Collection

The research team and the facilitators worked together in a series of workshop days to isolate and describe the deliberate acts of facilitation (DAFs) used by the facilitators and to explore the decision-making processes that underpinned their in-the-moment choices. Transcripts of conversations were used as a stimulus for discussion, and new scenarios were explored through role-play. Think-aloud responses and metacognitive reflections by the facilitators were recorded and analyzed. The data collection phase was collegial, and co-constructed, in order to deeply understand the facilitators' practice.

Data Analysis

Data in this study comprised transcripts of facilitation conversations, metacognitive reflections on conversations, and emerging descriptions of DAFs that had been jointly identified by the facilitators and researchers. Data were analyzed through an iterative process of narrative construction and critique. Discussion from the workshop days was used to create narratives and annotated transcripts that were shared back to the group for analysis and critique. An initial model of DAFs was co-constructed through this process and fed back to the PL initiative's wider team for trialing and commentary.

Strengths and Limitations

The co-construction of knowledge between facilitators and researchers was a strength of this study. The aim of the researchers was to make the facilitators' highly effective thinking and acts of facilitation available to others for PL. The facilitators' skills and knowledge were largely invisible to others because their practice occurred in schools, without other facilitators present, and because many of the highly sophisticated choices they were making were taken for granted or invisible to an observer or transcript reader. This study was limited by its small number of participants and because the co-construction of ideas is inevitably subjective. The data gathering was limited to perspectives from the facilitators and did not include school leaders. Data were also based on the participants' recall of significant conversations and actions rather than observations of them in action. These limitations led to the design of a larger project to pursue these ideas further.

What We Found

In terms of the model and tree metaphor in this book, this study provided the first iteration of the leaves of the tree: the DAFs. It also helped us to develop our definition of adaptive expertise and to explore the methodology of using annotated transcripts of leadership development conversations to uncover adaptive expertise in facilitation.

Facilitation in Action—the Main Study

The facilitation-in-action study was the key source of data for the model and metaphor presented in this book. This study combined two very productive elements of the DAFs study that it grew from: (1) the use of transcripts of facilitator practice as a key data source and (2) embedding the co-construction of meaning and checking of interpretations with the participants into the research design.

Six facilitators took part in this study. None of them had taken part in the previous study. They were purposively selected and invited based on the improvement in student achievement observed in the schools that they worked in and the adaptive expertise they demonstrated in their practice according to their senior colleagues. Like the previous group of facilitators, they were experienced educators with many years of work in schools as leaders and as facilitators behind them. The facilitators worked in elementary, middle, and high schools.

The Research Questions

This study sought to answer the following questions:

▶ What does adaptive expertise look like in effective facilitation?

▶ What supports adaptive expertise in facilitation and makes it possible?

▶ In what ways do DAFs promote the development of adaptive expertise in school leaders?

Data Collection

This study was rooted in authentic facilitator practice rather than based on recall of practice and generic discussion of effectiveness. It used leadership development conversations between facilitators and school leaders as the basis for interviews and transcript analysis. The data collection proceeded through six phases (described next) for each facilitator-school pairing. Three facilitators provided data for two schools, so there were nine complete sets of data in the study.

Each set of data began with an audio recorded and transcribed leadership development conversation between the facilitator and the school's leaders with whom they worked. These conversations ranged from fifteen minutes to one hour and twenty minutes, with most being between forty-five minutes and an hour long. These conversations were transcribed promptly and returned to the facilitator, who annotated them to identify excerpts that were particular decision points for them. Three follow-up interviews occurred. First, there was a short phone interview between the facilitator and a researcher to obtain immediate impressions about the conversation, its purpose, and context. Next, there was an extended face-to-face interview between the facilitator and a researcher, centered on the annotated transcript of the conversation and exploring how the facilitator aimed to develop adaptive expertise. The third interview was an extended interview of about an hour between a researcher and the school leader to understand their responses to the facilitator's choices and actions and how these did or didn't help them develop adaptive expertise.

Data Analysis

Data analysis consisted of an inductive descriptive approach, grounded in the data, followed by a deductive analysis based on definitions of adaptive expertise from the literature. Initial analysis identified themes in the facilitator-leader interactions with subsequent analyses developing these into a framework of adaptive expertise. A team of three researchers each worked independently with a complete set of data relating to one facilitator, building a case study of that facilitator. Researchers then exchanged data sets and case analyses and searched for confirming and disconfirming evidence and examples. The cases were then combined through a process of nomination and confirmation of key characteristics.

As with the previous study, the expertise of the facilitators was sought to test our interpretations and assumptions. Two full-day meetings were held for the research team and the facilitators. At these meetings the researchers presented their tentative themes and conclusions, and the facilitators questioned them, corrected them, and added to them. Further examples from their practice were suggested. Alternative explanations were explored.

Strengths and Limitations

The strengths of this study were that it began with authentic examples of facilitation practice and included the voices of the school leader participants, so we could better understand how the facilitation was received and processed in schools. Focusing on an artifact of practice allowed us to explore the adaptive expertise of the facilitators in depth. The study was limited by its small number of participants. The findings are interpretations of qualitative data. Validity and reliability were enhanced by including the school leaders' perspectives in the data and by checking our interpretations with the participants. The study's findings were used extensively by the PL initiative, providing further evidence of their relevance and usefulness.

What We Found

This study established the roots and trunk of the tree metaphor. Through the analysis we clarified and defined the orientations and commitments that permeated through all the decisions made by facilitators in their work with school leaders and recognized that these had a qualitatively different nature to the DAFs. From this insight we built and tested the tree metaphor as a way to understand the complex nature of adaptive expertise in facilitation. We proposed that developing the roots of the tree was a high-leverage way to improve facilitator practice as the roots provide the basis for deploying the DAFs.

A key element that emerged from this study was linguistic and cultural responsiveness (LCR). While responsiveness is clearly at the heart of adaptive expertise, considering the role of culture and language in how we respond was a new layer of thinking that emerged from this study. We therefore decided to investigate further what LCR might mean in facilitation and how it fit into the idea of adaptive expertise.

Linguistic and Cultural Responsiveness in Facilitation—Building Skills and Knowledge

In this study the expert practice of a lead facilitator was used to explore what LCR in facilitation might be like. The lead facilitator was a noted academic and leader whose work in bilingualism and Pasifika education was well known and deeply respected. She worked with a group of teachers, looking at how to use the language resources of bilingual children in Grade 1 classrooms. Transcripts of conversations between the lead facilitator and individual teachers were used as the basis for conversations with a group of eleven volunteer facilitators in a two-session PL opportunity. The eleven volunteer facilitators also participated in focus group discussions with members of the research team after the learning opportunity to explore what LCR means in facilitation practice.

The Research Questions

This study sought to answer the following questions:

- ▶ What does effective PL facilitation focused on the development of LCR pedagogies look like?
- ▶ What do PL facilitators need to learn to be able to facilitate effectively for LCR in schools?

Data Collection

The data sources for this study were transcripts of the lead facilitator working with Grade 1 teachers, an interview with the lead facilitator about her practice, transcripts of the PL sessions with the 11 facilitators, and transcripts of two focus group discussions between the research team and the 11 facilitators.

Data Analysis

This study drew on a range of sources and was made complex by the multilayered nature of the work. In order to continue our commitment to working from authentic examples of practice, transcripts of facilitation conversations played a dual role in this study: exemplifying effective LCR facilitation and providing a stimulus for discussion with facilitators about their practices and what could be learned from the transcripts.

An initial inductive thematic analysis across the data sources was complemented by a deductive analysis using two frameworks: (1) the tree metaphor (in particular the roots of the tree as orientations and commitments) and (2) a framework for Pasifika success (Si'ilata, Wendt Samu, & Siteine, 2017).

Strengths and Limitations

LCR is often discussed, but finding and using concrete examples of expertise in this area is less frequent. The study is limited by the small number of participants and the brief time available for the PL experience. Nonetheless, it is a useful start on a very important area.

What We Found

By exploring exemplary practice across two settings and working collaboratively to explore what LCR might be in facilitation for adaptive expertise, we enriched our model and metaphor. Deeper understanding of the implications of LCR for our claims in the model led to some alterations to the wording of the roots and additional points to consider in our descriptions. We also looked at fundamental ways in which the model linked to Pasifika education aspirations and worldview. These findings are less relevant for an international audience but were important in our local context.

Understanding the Nature and Impact of Perceptions of Risk

The rationale for this strand of research was that when people engage in PL and educational change, either as leaders, facilitators, or teachers, there is a significant emotional element involved. Central to this emotional element of change is a possible perception of risk that is inherent in change. People have a perception of risk when they perceive the possibility of losing something they value if they engage in change. Risk taking is therefore an important behavior to understand in an environment of change where there is some degree of uncertainty about the future. In the first year we developed and conducted a risk questionnaire to ascertain educators' perceived risk in PL. As a result of finding perceived risk affecting educators' actions, we explored facilitators' perceptions of risk in their work with those involved in the adaptive expertise studies described previously.

The Research Questions

The study sought to answer the following questions:

- What do leaders, PL facilitators, and teachers perceive as a risk when engaging in PL for educational change?
- What factors influence perceptions of risk for leaders, PL facilitators, and teachers engaging with change?
- What can leaders and professional developers do to reduce perceptions of risk for teachers?

Data Collection

The participants in the initial study were 296 classroom teachers, 41 PL facilitators, and 68 school leaders who were a representative sample from the larger project already discussed. Each participant completed a questionnaire developed specifically for this research that identified four overarching factors regarding the extent to which they found specific tasks of PL a risk and the extent to which they were willing to engage in them. See Teo and Le Fevre (2016) for further information.

Semistructured interviews with a representative sample from the questionnaire of nineteen teachers, six school leaders, and twelve PL facilitators probed the underlying reasons for their perceptions of risk. In subsequent years we deliberately explored the experiences, feelings, and views of the facilitators involved in the earlier research for their perceptions of risk as they worked with LCR contexts.

Data Analysis

A quantitative analysis of questionnaire data was undertaken. Participants' responses to a six-point Likert scale regarding the extent to which they perceived something as a risk ranged from 1 = no risk to 6 = extreme risk. Their responses to willingness to engage in practices ranged from 1 = not at all willing to 6 = extremely willing. Throughout the work, three researchers used qualitative thematic analysis of interview transcript data. An inductive or deductive approach was taken, moving between theory and practice.

Strengths and Limitations

An extensive questionnaire development process enabled the development of a questionnaire with four distinctive factors, and the number of participants willing to take part in the questionnaire part of the study enabled patterns of risk perception to be identified. However, only a sample of these could be interviewed due to the scope and funding of the study.

The ongoing analysis of facilitators' interview data enabled the team to surface perceptions of risk in facilitating PL and integrate this knowledge into the adaptive expertise model.

What We Found

Quantitative analyses of questionnaire data provided a consistent pattern whereby the greater the perceived risk a person had of a practice of change, the less willing they were to engage in that practice. Just as teachers have a central role in influencing the nature of the learning environment for their students, leaders and PL facilitators have an important role in shaping the learning environment for teachers. Qualitative analyses of interviews revealed that PL facilitators and school leaders can reduce perceptions of risk for teachers. They can reduce teachers' feelings of uncertainty and vulnerability by developing a shared, clear understanding of the purpose and motivation for change, providing for the development of necessary knowledge and skills, and providing a supportive environment for risk taking. These ideas have been incorporated into the deliberate act of navigating perceptions of risk in the tree model.

We also found patterns in facilitators' experiences as they deliberately challenged themselves to work in different ways within the LCR context. Initially they perceived high risk when challenging the beliefs of others, clarifying purpose, and linking to LCR frameworks. Practices they were familiar with, such as using evidence, were associated with lesser risk. By the end of our research, facilitators reported that perceived risk lessened as their knowledge deepened.

Summary

The research that underpins the model and metaphor in this book built on existing scholarship on adaptive expertise and sought to extend this into what adaptive expertise in facilitation might mean and what its effects are. Through a series of connected studies, over a period of five years, we worked closely with a large group of PL facilitators to build knowledge about adaptive expertise in working with school leaders on improving outcomes for learners. Our findings are summarized and exemplified in the tree metaphor and facilitation model that are presented in this book. The version presented here has been iteratively developed through cycles of research, feedback from practitioners, use in the field, and further research.

References

Argyris, C., & Schön, D. A. (1974). *Theory in practice: Increasing professional effectiveness.* Oxford, England: Jossey-Bass.

Asterhan, C. (2013). Epistemic and interpersonal dimensions of peer argumentation: Conceptualization and quantitative assessment. In M. Baker, J. Andriessen, & S. Jarvela (Eds.), *Affective learning together: Social and emotional dimensions of collaborative learning* (pp. 261–281). Oxon, England: Routledge.

Aven, T., & Renn, O. (2009). On risk defined as an event where the outcome is uncertain. *Journal of Risk Research, 12*, 1–11.

Baker, M., Andriessen, J., & Jarvela, S. (Eds.). (2013). *Affective learning together: Social and emotional dimensions of collaborative learning.* Oxon, England: Routledge.

Bandura, A. (2001). Social cognitive theory: An agentic perspective. *Annual Review of Psychology, 52*, 1–26.

Berry, A. (2008). *Tensions in teaching about teaching: Understanding practice as a teacher educator.* Dordrecht, The Netherlands: Springer.

Biesta, G., Priestly, M., & Robinson, S. (2015). The role of beliefs in teacher agency. *Teachers and Teaching: Theory and Practice, 21*, 624–640.

Bishop, R. (2010). Effective teaching for indigenous and minoritized students. *Procedia Social and Behavioral Sciences, 7*, 57–62.

Blank, A., Houkamau, C., & Kingi, H. (2016). *Unconscious bias and education: A comparative study of Maori and African American students* (Report). Wellington, New Zealand: Oranui Diversity Leadership. Retrieved from http://www.oranui.co.nz/images/oranui_reports/unconscious-bias-and-education.pdf

Boekaerts, M. (2010). The crucial role of motivation and emotion in classroom learning. In H. Dumont, D. Istance, & F. Benavides (Eds.), *The nature of learning: Using research to inspire practice* (pp. 91–111). Paris, France: OECD Publishing.

Bransford, J., Brown, A., & Cocking, R. (2000). *How people learn: Brain, mind, experience and school.* Washington DC: National Academies Press.

Bransford, J., Mosborg, S., Copland, M., Honig, M., Nelson, H., Gawel, D., . . . Vye, N. (2010). Adaptive people and adaptive systems: Issues of learning and design. In A. Hargreaves, A. Lieberman, M. Fullan, & D. Hopkins (Eds.), *Second international handbook of educational change* (pp. 825–855). Dordrecht, The Netherlands: Springer.

Bryk, A. S., Gomez, L. M., Grunow, A., & LeMahieu, P. G. (2015). *Learning to improve: How America's schools can get better at getting better.* Cambridge, MA: Harvard Education Press.

Bryk, A. S., & Schneider, B. L. (2002). *Trust in schools: A core resource for improvement.* New York, NY: Russell Sage Foundation.

Bryk, A. S., Sebring, P. B., Kerbow, D., Rollow, S., & Easton, J. Q. (1998). *Charting Chicago school reform: Democratic localism as a lever of change.* Boulder, CO: Westview Press.

Butler, D., Schnellert, B., & Perry, N. (2016). *Developing self-regulated learners.* Toronto, Canada: Pearson.

Butler, D., & Winne, P. (1995). Feedback and self-regulated learning: A synthesis. *Review of Educational Research, 65*, 245–281.

Campbell, C., Lieberman, A., & Yashkina, A. (2018). Teacher-led professional collaboration and systemic capacity building. In A. Harris, M. Jones, & J. B. Huffman (Eds.), *Teachers leading educational reform: The power of professional learning communities* (pp. 72–85). London, England: Routledge.

Chi, M. T. H. (1996). Constructing self-explanations and scaffolded explanations in tutoring. *Applied Cognitive Psychology, 10*, 33–49.

Chrispeels, J. H., & Gonzalez, M. (2006). The challenge of systemic change in complex educational systems: A district model to scale up reform. In A. Harris & J. H. Chrispeels (Eds.), *Improving schools and educational systems* (pp. 241–273). London, England: Routledge.

Coburn, C. E. (2001). Collective sensemaking about reading: How teachers mediate reading policy in their professional communities. *American Educational Research Association, 23*, 145–170.

Cochran-Smith, M., Ell, F., Ludlow, L., Grudnoff, L., & Aitken, G. (2014). The challenge and promise of complexity theory for teacher education research. *Teachers College Record, 116*, 1–38.

Cochran-Smith, M., & Lytle, S. L. (2009). *Inquiry as stance: Practitioner research for the next generation.* New York, NY: Teachers College Press.

Colton, A. B., Langer, G. M., & Goff, L. S. (2015). Create a safe space to learn. *Journal of Staff Development, 36*, 40–45, 66.

Cuban, L. (2015). *Fixing schools again and again.* Retrieved from https://larrycubanwordpress.com/2015/07/03/fixing-schools-again-and-again

Damşa, C., Ludvigsen, S., & Andriessen, J. (2013). Knowledge co-construction—Epistemic consensus or relational assent? In M. Baker, J. Andriessen, & S. Jarvela (Eds.), *Affective learning together: Social and emotional dimensions of collaborative learning* (pp. 106–129). Oxon, England: Routledge.

Darling-Hammond, L., & Bransford, J. (Eds.). (2005). *Preparing teachers for a changing world: What teachers should learn and be able to do.* San Francisco, CA: Jossey-Bass.

Datnow, A. (2011). Collaboration and contrived collegiality: Revisiting Hargreaves in the age of accountability. *Journal of Educational Change, 12,* 147–158. doi:10.1007/s10833-011-9154-1

Donohoo, J. (2016). *Collective efficacy: How educators' beliefs impact student learning.* Thousand Oaks, CA: Corwin.

Donohoo, J. (2017). Collective teacher efficacy research: Implications for professional learning. *Journal of Professional Capital and Community, 2,* 101–116. Retrieved from https://doi.org/10.1108/ JPCC-10-2016-0027

Donohoo, J., Hattie, J., & Eells, R. (2018). The power of collective efficacy. *Educational Leadership, 75,* 41–44.

Donohoo, J., & Velasco, M. (2016). *The transformative power of collaborative inquiry. Realizing change in schools and classrooms.* Thousand Oaks, CA: Corwin.

Dumont, H., Istance, D., & Benavides, F. (Eds.). (2010). *The nature of learning: Using research to inspire practice.* Paris, France: OECD.

Dumont, H., Istance, D., & Benavides, F. (Eds.). (2012). *The nature of learning: Using research to inspire practice—Practitioner guide.* Paris, France: OECD, Centre for Educational Research and Innovation. Retrieved from http://www.oecd.org/edu/ceri/50300814.pdf

Earl, L. M., & Katz, S. (2006). *Leading schools in a data-rich world: Harnessing data for school improvement.* Thousand Oaks, CA: Corwin.

Earl, L. M., & Katz, S. (2010). Creating a culture of inquiry: Harnessing data for professional learning. In A. Blankstein, P. Houston, & R. Cole (Eds.), *Data-enhanced leadership* (pp. 9–30). Thousand Oaks, CA: Corwin.

Earl, L., & Timperley, H. (2016). *Embedding evaluative thinking as an essential component of successful innovation* (Seminar Series 257). Melbourne, Australia: Centre for Strategic Education.

Edmondson, A. C. (1999). Psychological safety and learning behavior in work teams. *Administrative Science Quarterly, 44,* 350–383. doi:10.2307/2666999

Elmore, R. F. (2004). *School reform from the inside out: Policy, practice, and performance.* Cambridge, MA: Harvard Education Press.

Flavell, J. H. (1979). Metacognition and cognitive monitoring: A new area of cognitive-developmental inquiry. *American Psychologist, 34,* 906–911.

Forsyth, P. B., Adams, C. M., & Hoy, W. K. (2011). *Collective trust: Why schools can't improve without it.* New York, NY: Teachers College Press.

Fullan, M. (2009). Have theory, will travel: A theory of action for system change. In A. Hargreaves & M. Fullan (Eds.), *Change wars* (pp. 275–293). Bloomington, IN: Solution Tree.

Fullan, M., & Quinn, J. (2016). *Coherence: The right drivers in action for schools, districts, and systems.* Thousand Oaks, CA: Corwin.

Gilbert, J. (2015). *Leading in collaborative, complex education systems.* Paper commissioned by the Education Council of New Zealand, Wellington.

Guskey, T. R. (1986). Staff development and the process of teacher change. *American Educational Research Association, 15,* 5–12.

Hare, W. (2006). Why open-mindedness matters. *Think, 5,* 7–16.

Hare, W. (2009). What open-mindedness requires. *Skeptical Inquirer, 33,* 36–39.

Hargreaves, A. (1998). The emotional practice of teaching. *Teaching and Teacher Education, 14,* 834–854. doi:10.1080/1363243042000266936

Hargreaves, A., & Fullan, M. (2012). *Professional capital: Transforming teaching in every school.* New York, NY: Teachers College Press.

Hargreaves, A., & O'Connor, M. T. (2018). *Collaborative professionalism.* Thousand Oaks, CA: Corwin.

Hargreaves, A., & Shirley, D. (2018). *Leading from the middle: Spreading learning, well-being and identity across Ontario: Council of Ontario Directors of Education report.* Ontario, Canada: Council of Ontario Directors of Education. Retrieved from http://ccsli.ca/downloads/2018-Leading_From_the_Middle_Final-EN.pdf

Hatano, G., & Inagaki, K. (1986). Two courses of expertise. In H. Stevenson, H. Azama, & K. Hakuta (Eds.), *Child development and education in Japan* (pp. 262–272). New York, NY: Freeman.

Heifetz, R., & Linsky, M. (2017). *Leadership on the line: Staying alive through the dangers of leading* (Rev. ed). Boston, MA: Harvard Business School Press.

Heifetz, R. A. (2010, Spring). Adaptive work. *The Journal Kansas Leadership Center,* 72–77.

Helal, M., & Coelli, M. B. (2016). *How principals affect schools* (Working Paper #18/16). Retrieved from https://papers.ssrn.com/sol3/Data_Integrity_Notice.cfm?abid=2788316

Istance, D., & Dumont, H. (2010). Future directions for learning environments in the 21st century. In H. Dumont, D. Istance, & F. Benavides (Eds.), *The nature of learning* (pp. 317–338). Paris, France: OECD Publishing.

Jensen, B., Sonnemann, J., Roberts-Hull, K., & Hunter, A. (2016). *Beyond PD: Teacher professional learning in high-performing systems* (Australian ed.). Washington, DC: National Center on Education and the Economy.

Katz, S., & Dack, L. I. (2013). *Intentional interruption: Breaking down learning barriers to transform professional practice.* Thousand Oaks, CA: Corwin.

Katz, S., Earl, L. M., & Jaafar, S. B. (2009). *Building and connecting learning communities: The power of networks for school improvement.* Thousand Oaks, CA: Corwin.

Korthagen, F. (2001). Building a realistic teacher education program. In F. Korthagen, J. Kessels, B. Koster, B. Lagerwerf, & T. Wubbels (Eds.), *Linking practice and theory: The pedagogy of realistic teacher education* (pp. 69–87). Mahwah, NJ: Lawrence Erlbaum.

Lai, M., Timperley, H., & McNaughton, S. (2010). Theories for improvement and sustainability. In H. Timperley & J. Parr (Eds.), *Weaving evidence, inquiry and standards to build better schools* (pp. 53–70). Wellington: New Zealand Council for Educational Research Press.

Le Fevre, D. M. (2010). Changing TACK: Talking about change knowledge for professional learning. In H. S. Timperley & J. Parr (Eds.), *Weaving evidence, inquiry and standards to build better schools* (pp. 71–91). Wellington: New Zealand Council for Educational Research Press.

Le Fevre, D. M. (2014). Barriers to implementing pedagogical change: The role of teachers' perceptions of risk. *Teaching and Teacher Education, 38,* 56–64.

Le Fevre, D. M., Robinson, V. M. J., & Sinnema, C. E. L. (2014). Genuine inquiry: Widely espoused but rarely enacted. *Educational Management Administration and Leadership, 43,* 883–899.

Le Fevre, D. M., Timperley, H., & Ell, F. (2015). Curriculum and pedagogy: The future of teacher professional learning and the development of adaptive expertise. In D. Wyse, L. Hayward, & J. Pandya (Eds.), *The SAGE handbook of curriculum, pedagogy, and assessment* (pp. 309–324). Thousand Oaks, CA: Sage.

Levin, T., & Wadmany, R. (2006). Teachers' beliefs and practices in technology-based classrooms: A developmental view. *Journal of Research on Technology in Education, 39,* 157–181.

Little, J. W., Gearhart, M., Curry, G. M., & Kafka, J. (2003). Looking at student work for teacher learning, teacher community, and school reform. *Phi Delta Kappan, 85,* 184–192.

Marris, P. (1986). *Loss and change* (Rev. ed.). London, England: Routledge & Kegan Paul.

McKenzie, K. B., & Scheurich, J. J. (2004). Equity traps: A useful construct for preparing principals to lead schools that are successful with racially diverse students. *Educational Administration Quarterly, 40,* 601–632.

McKenzie, R., & Singleton, H. (2009, October). *Moving from Pasifika immersion to Palangi Primary school. Knowing the learner is precious.* Paper presented at the Exploring Effective Transitions Conference, Hamilton, New Zealand.

Mead, H. R. M. (2012). *Understanding mātauranga Māori* in Conversations on Mātauranga Māori. Retrieved from http://www.nzqa.govt.nz/assets/Maori/ConversationsMMv6AW-web.pdf

Nelson, T. H., Slavit, D., Perkins, M., & Hathorn, T. (2008). A culture of collaborative inquiry: Learning to develop and support professional learning communities. *Teachers College Record, 110,* 1269–1303.

Opfer, D. V., & Pedder, D. (2011). The lost promise of teacher professional development in England. *European Journal of Teacher Education, 34,* 3–24. doi:10.1080/02619768.2010.534131

Organisation for Economic Co-operation and Development. (2012). *Equity and quality in education: Supporting disadvantaged students and schools.* Paris, France: OECD Publishing. Retrieved from http://dx.doi.org/10.1787/9789264130852-en

Patton, M. Q. (2011). *Developmental evaluation: Applying complexity concepts to enhance innovation and use.* New York, NY: Guilford Press.

Pellegrino, J., & Hilton, M. (Eds.). (2012). *Education for life and work: Developing transferable knowledge and skills in the 21st century.* Washington, DC: National Academies Press.

Poekert, P. (2011). The pedagogy of facilitation: Teacher inquiry as professional development in a Florida elementary school. *Professional Development in Education, 37,* 19–38. doi:10.1080/19415251003737309

Ponticell, J. A. (2003). Enhancers and inhibitors of teacher risk taking: A case study. *Peabody Journal of Education, 78,* 5–24.

Richardson, V. (1992). The agenda-setting dilemma in a constructivist staff development process. *Teaching and Teacher Education, 8,* 287–300.

Richardson, V. (1996). The role of attitudes and beliefs in learning to teach. In J. Sikula (Ed.), *Handbook of research on teacher education* (2nd ed., pp. 102–119). New York, NY: Macmillan.

Robinson, V., Hohepa, M., & Lloyd, C. (2009). *School leadership and student outcomes: What works and why? Best evidence synthesis iteration.* Wellington, New Zealand: Ministry of Education.

Robinson, V., & Lai, M. K. (2006). *Practitioner research for educators: A guide to improving classrooms and schools.* Thousand Oaks, CA: Corwin.

Robinson, V. M. J. (2011). *Student-centered leadership.* San Francisco, CA: Jossey-Bass.

Robinson, V. M. J. (2018). *Reduce change to increase improvement.* Thousand Oaks, CA: Corwin.

Robinson, V. M. J., Le Fevre, D. M., & Sinnema, C. E. L. (Eds.). (2017). *Open-to-learning™ leadership: How to build trust while tackling tough issues.* Melbourne, Australia: Hawker Brownlow Education.

Robinson, V. M. J., Lloyd, C., & Rowe, K. J. (2008). The impact of leadership on student outcomes: An analysis of the differential effects of leadership type. *Educational Administration Quarterly, 44*, 635–674. doi:10.1177/0013161X08321509

Robinson, V. M. J., Sinnema, C. E., & Le Fevre, D. (2014). From persuasion to learning: An intervention to improve leaders' response to disagreement. *Leadership and Policy in Schools, 13*, 260–296.

Schildkamp, K., Lai, M. K., & Earl, E. (Eds). (2014). *Data-based decision making in education: Challenges and opportunities.* Dordrecht, The Netherlands: Springer.

Schön, D. (1983). *The reflective practitioner: How professionals think in action.* San Francisco, CA: Jossey-Bass.

Si'ilata, R. (2014). *Va'a Tele: Pasifika learners riding the success wave on linguistically and culturally responsive pedagogies.* (Unpublished doctoral dissertation). University of Auckland, Auckland, New Zealand.

Si'ilata, R. K., Wendt Samu, T., & Siteine, A. (2017). The Va'atele framework: Redefining and transforming Pasifika education. In E. McKinley & L. Tuhiwai Smith (Eds.), *The handbook of indigenous education.* Singapore: Springer. doi:10.1007/978-981-10-1839-8_34-1

Sleeter, C. E. (2001). Preparing teachers for culturally diverse schools: Research and the overwhelming presence of whiteness. *Journal of Teacher Education, 52*, 94–106.

Sleeter, C. E., & Montecinos, C. (1999). Forging partnerships for multicultural teacher education. In S. May (Ed.), *Critical multiculturalism: Rethinking multicultural and antiracist education* (pp. 124–150). Philadelphia, Pennsylvania: Falmer Press.

Stoll, L., Fink, D., & Earl, L. (2003). *It's about learning (and it's about time): What's in it for schools?* London, England: Routledge.

Teo, T., & Le Fevre, D. (2016). The development and validation of the teachers' perception of risk scale (TPRS) in educational change. *Current Psychology, 36*, 649–656. doi:10.1007/s12144-016-9453-z

Timperley, H. (2008). Teacher professional learning and development. *Educational Practices Series-18.* Geneva, Switzerland: International Academy of Education & International Bureau of Education.

Timperley, H. (2011). Leading teachers' professional learning. In J. Robertson & H. S. Timperley (Eds.), *Leadership and learning* (pp. 118–130). London, England: Sage.

Timperley, H., & Alton-Lee, A. (2008). Reframing teacher professional learning: An alternative policy approach to strengthening outcomes for diverse learners. *Review of Research in Education, 32*, 328–369.

Timperley, H., Kaser, L., & Halbert, J. (2014). *A framework for transforming learning in schools: Innovation and the spiral of inquiry.* Melbourne, Australia: Centre for Strategic Education.

Timperley, H., McNaughton, S., Lai, M., Hohepa, M., Parr, J., & Dingle, R. (2010). Evaluative capability requires using evidence throughout teaching and learning cycles. In H. Timperley & J. Parr (Eds.), *Weaving evidence, inquiry and standards to build better schools* (pp. 25–49). Wellington: New Zealand Council for Educational Research Press.

Timperley, H., & Robertson, J. (2011). Establishing platforms for leadership and learning. In J. Robertson & H. Timperley (Eds.), *Leadership and learning* (pp. 3–12). London, England: Sage.

Timperley, H., Wilson, A., Barrar, H., & Fung, I. (2007). *Teacher professional learning and development: Best evidence synthesis iteration.* Wellington, New Zealand: Ministry of Education.

Timperley, H. S., & Robinson, V. M. J. (2001). Achieving school improvement through challenging and changing teachers' schema. *Journal of Educational Change, 2*, 281–300.

Twyford, K. (2016). *Risk or resistance: Understanding teachers' perceptions of risk in professional learning* (Unpublished doctoral dissertation). University of Auckland, Auckland, New Zealand.

Twyford, K., Le Fevre, D., & Timperley, H. (2017). The influence of risk and uncertainty on teachers' responses to professional learning and development. *Journal of Professional Capital and Community, 2*, 86–100. Retrieved from https://doi.org/10.1108/JPCC-10-2016-0028

Wajnryb, R. (1996). The pragmatics of feedback: Supervision as a clash-of-goals between message and face. In A. Yarrow, J. Millwater, S. De Vries, & D. Creedy (Eds.), *PEPE research monograph: No. 1* (pp. 135–154). Brisbane, Australia: Queensland University of Technology.

Zimmerman, B. (2002). Becoming a self-regulated learner: An overview. *Theory Into Practice, 41*, 64–70.

Research Reports

Ell, F., Hawke, J., Reeves, J., Runga, C., Shepherd, B., Timperley, H., & Twyford, K. (2014). *CPL: Acts of facilitation that make a difference* (CPL Report). Auckland, New Zealand: Commissioning Body: Consortium for Professional Learning.

Le Fevre, D. M., Ell, F., Timperley, H., Twyford, K., & Mayo, S. (2015). *Developing adaptive expertise: The practice of effective facilitators* (CPL Report). Auckland, New Zealand: Commissioning Body: Consortium for Professional Learning.

Le Fevre, D. M., Si'ilata, R., Timperley, H., Twyford, K., Mayo, S., & Ell, F. (2016). *Developing linguistically and culturally responsive practice* (CPL Report). Auckland, New Zealand: Commissioning Body: Consortium for Professional Learning.

Le Fevre, D. M., & Twyford, K. (2012). *Perceptions of risk in professional learning for change: Implications for facilitation and leadership* (CPL Report). Auckland, New Zealand: Commissioning Body: Consortium for Professional Learning.

Le Fevre, D. M., Twyford, K., & Sinclair, A. (2013). *Facilitators' perceptions of risk in professional learning for change* (CPL Report). Auckland, New Zealand: Commissioning Body: Consortium for Professional Learning.

Si'ilata, R., Le Fevre, D. M., Ell, F., Timperley, H., Twyford, K., & Mayo, S. (2015). *Adaptive expertise in the facilitation of linguistic and cultural responsiveness* (CPL Report). Auckland, New Zealand: Commissioning Body: Consortium for Professional Learning.

Index

A SAGE Publishing Company

CORWIN HAS ONE MISSION: to enhance education through intentional professional learning.

We build long-term relationships with our authors, educators, clients, and associations who partner with us to develop and continuously improve the best evidence-based practices that establish and support lifelong learning.

THE PROFESSIONAL LEARNING ASSOCIATION

Learning Forward is a nonprofit, international membership association of learning educators committed to one vision in K–12 education: Excellent teaching and learning every day. To realize that vision, Learning Forward pursues its mission to build the capacity of leaders to establish and sustain highly effective professional learning. Information about membership, services, and products is available from www.learningforward.org.

Solutions YOU WANT | Experts YOU TRUST | Results YOU NEED

EVENTS

>>> **INSTITUTES**

Corwin Institutes provide large regional events where educators collaborate with peers and learn from industry experts. Prepare to be recharged and motivated!

corwin.com/institutes

ON-SITE PD

>>> **ON-SITE PROFESSIONAL LEARNING**

Corwin on-site PD is delivered through high-energy keynotes, practical workshops, and custom coaching services designed to support knowledge development and implementation.

corwin.com/pd

>>> **PROFESSIONAL DEVELOPMENT RESOURCE CENTER**

The PD Resource Center provides school and district PD facilitators with the tools and resources needed to deliver effective PD.

corwin.com/pdrc

ONLINE

>>> **ADVANCE**

Designed for K–12 teachers, Advance offers a range of online learning options that can qualify for graduate-level credit and apply toward license renewal.

corwin.com/advance

Contact a PD Advisor at (800) 831-6640 or visit www.corwin.com for more information